T0367549

THE HEART SUTRA

THE HEART SUTRA

An Oral Teaching by
Geshe Sonam Rinchen

Translated and edited by
Ruth Sonam

SNOW LION
Boulder

Snow Lion
An imprint of Shambhala Publications, Inc.
4720 Walnut Street
Boulder, Colorado 80301
www.shambhala.com

The thangka image of Shakyamuni Buddha that appears on the front cover is
courtesy of the Rubin Foundation (www.himalayanart.org).

The author and translator would like to thank editor Susan Kyser for her invaluable
assistance.

Printed in the United States of America

Library of Congress Cataloging-in-Publication Data

Sonam Rinchen, 1933–
The Heart Sutra: an oral teaching / by Geshe Sonam Rinchen; translated and edited
by Ruth Sonam.
p. cm.
Includes bibliographical references.
ISBN 978-1-55939-201-3
1. Tripiṭaka. Sūtrapiṭaka. Prajñāpāramitā. Hṛdaya—Commentaries. I. Sonam, Ruth,
1943– II. Tripiṭaka. Sūtrapiṭaka. Prajñāpāramitā. Hṛdaya. English & Tibetan. III.
Title.
BQ1967 .S64 2003
294.3'85—dc21
2003012450

CONTENTS

Introduction   1

The Perfection of Wisdom Sutras   11

The Heart Sutra   17

The Prologue   27

The Question   35

Form Is Empty   43

The Eight Aspects   51

No Conventional Phenomena   55

The Mantra   69

The Conclusion and Colophon   83

The Root Text: *The Heart Sutra*   89

The Tibetan Text   95

Notes   99

Source Readings   127

INTRODUCTION

Throughout the world education is seen as a key to progress and success, and considerable amounts of money are spent on providing educational facilities. But buildings and hardware are not of much use without good teachers and interested students. Knowledge and understanding are the foundation for all accomplishments. The great Indian master Nagarjuna[1] said:

> The root of all seen and unseen
> Qualities is knowledge.
> Therefore to accomplish both
> Hold knowledge firmly.

Seen or visible good qualities are those we aspire to develop in this life, while the presently invisible ones are those we may hope to possess in the future.

Recognizing just how crucial it is to have reliable knowledge, particularly concerning the nature of reality, will stimulate our interest to discover more about our own condition and the world in which we live. Normally we don't spend much time thinking about how things actually exist, but understanding the nature of reality has the power eventually to free us from suffering.

Since we are concerned here with something very subtle, we need guidance from a well-qualified and compassionate spiritual teacher who is fully capable of explaining how we can gain this knowledge. For understanding derived from thinking about and meditating on the nature of reality we must first hear and read about it sufficiently. Mere factual knowledge, however, is not enough to bring about a radical change in our outlook. Only understanding that has been integrated can lead to such a shift.

The Buddha is said to have given eighty-four thousand different teachings, the essence of which is contained in the Perfection of Wisdom sutras, of which the *Heart Sutra*[2] is the most concise version. The Perfection of Wisdom sutras explain the most subtle and fundamental way in which things exist. Without understanding this level of reality the obstructions formed by our disturbing emotions and their seeds and the obstructions to knowledge of all phenomena formed primarily by the imprints of these disturbing emotions cannot be removed. Maitreya points this out in his *Sublime Continuum:*[3]

> Through understanding and by no other means
> Can these be eliminated. For that reason
> Understanding is supreme. Its basis is hearing
> And therefore hearing is superlative.

Maitreya stresses that the basis for the understanding of reality is extensive exposure to the teachings. The following sutra passage reiterates this:

> Child of the lineage, if you have hearing, understanding will arise. If you have understanding, the disturbing emotions will be pacified. One who is without the disturbing emotions will not be harmed by demons.

Through hearing the teachings sufficiently understanding will arise, and through this the disturbing emotions will be pacified in such a way that no demonic forces can ever vanquish us again.

Although, of course, intelligence and a broad education are important, it is only through the crucial understanding of reality that we can free ourselves from the noxious influence of the disturbing emotions, which make our minds unpeaceful and uncontrolled. First we must fully recognize how the disturbing emotions affect us by watching what happens when they have the upper hand. Then we need to gain certainty that the correct understanding of reality will allow us to throw off their tyranny. With that conviction, a strong interest and urge to do so will arise quite naturally. We will ask who has successfully overcome the disturbing emotions by recognizing the way things exist at their most fundamental level and where that knowledge can be found.

It is said that after the Buddha attained enlightenment, he spoke the following words:

I have found something nectar-like: profound,
Peaceful, unelaborated, unproduced, the clear light.
Since none to whom I may explain it will understand,
In silence I shall remain hidden in the forest.

These words demonstrate five features of the nature body of an enlightened being, which is the emptiness of an enlightened being's mind. That emptiness is difficult to understand and thus is profound. It is the pacification of all the imprints of contaminated actions and of the disturbing emotions. It is free from all the elaborations of conceptuality and it is clear light in that it is devoid of all natural and adventitious stains. It is unproduced and lacks inherent existence at the beginning, intermediately, and at the end.

Since the Buddha realized that emptiness, the fundamental nature of things, is something very subtle, according to ordinary appearances, he hesitated to teach for forty days or so because of the danger that it might be misunderstood or overwhelm those of inferior intelligence and insufficient enthusiasm. For this reason the gods Indra and Brahma are said to have offered the Buddha a golden wheel with a thousand spokes,[4] fervently requesting him to teach about the nature of reality.

This indicates that one should not teach unless a specific request has been made. In Tibet a benefactor would request a particular teaching to be given publicly to benefit as many others as possible, but people did not take it for granted that they could attend. It was customary to ask the spiritual teacher for explicit permission. It is the spiritual teacher's responsibility to assess whether that teaching is suitable for those who have requested it.

Just as a medicinal potion can cure disease, those who find the clear light nectar-like emptiness can cure their disease of the disturbing emotions and the external and internal troubles that afflict them. Of course this doesn't mean that the moment one understands emptiness, the disturbing emotions instantly cease. Finding the right medicine is not enough. We must continue to take it until the treatment is complete. Similarly, once emptiness has been understood, we must gain greater and greater familiarity with it in order to experience its healing effects.

All that the Buddha taught was for the purpose of leading us directly or indirectly to this understanding—to help us gain it if we do not already have it and to strengthen and make it more stable once we have gained it. Although it is hard to arrive at the right understanding of emptiness and dependent arising, without it we cannot free ourselves from cyclic existence. It is the only and supreme means of overcoming the ignorance which is responsible for all our miseries.

In his *Four Hundred [Verses] on the Yogic Deeds of Bodhisattvas*, Aryadeva[5] says:

Correct perception [leads to] the supreme state,
Some perception to good rebirths.
The wise thus always expand their intelligence
To think about the inner nature.

Through familiarity with the direct understanding of reality we will reach the supreme state of enlightenment, but even some understanding will be of tremendous benefit. Aryadeva also says:

Those with little merit
Do not even doubt this teaching.
Entertaining just a doubt
Tears to tatters worldly existence.

Most of us never think about what is responsible for the suffering we experience and whether or not we see things as they really are. Just a suspicion that what great masters like Nagarjuna have said could be true—namely that all things are empty of intrinsic existence yet function in a completely satisfactory way—tears the first rent in the fabric of cyclic existence. Why does it have such a dramatic effect? By having that suspicion, even if we are not certain, we have briefly paid attention to reality, which begins the process of uprooting the cause of our suffering and may give us the incentive to probe more deeply and discover more about the fundamental nature of things.

In his commentary on Aryadeva's *Four Hundred*, Chandrakirti[6] cites an illustration of this. Once there was a ship's captain who was captured by an ogress and held prisoner on an island. She told him never to go to the south, not even to look in that direction. This naturally aroused his curiosity and made him all the more keen to know what lay to the south. One day he escaped her watchful eyes and walked as fast as he could to the southern part of the island, where he found Balahaka, the king of horses. He held on to Balahaka's mane and the magic horse bore him away from the island across the ocean to safety. Balahaka symbolizes the understanding of emptiness, which has the power to carry us beyond cyclic existence. Just holding on to a single hair of Balahaka's tail is enough for us to be carried across that ocean. In other words, by using even limited lines of reasoning to establish emptiness rather than the vast array presented in the Mahayana texts, we can free ourselves from cyclic existence.

In his *Praise for Dependent Arising* Je Tsongkhapa[7] says:

Whatever troubles of this world
Their root is ignorance. You taught
The insight which reverses it,
Dependent relativity.

Je Tsongkhapa says that everything the Buddha practiced before he attained enlightenment and the fruit of that practice were intended to relieve the woes of the world. "The world" here is used to translate the Tibetan *jigten* (*jig rten*), which means disintegrating basis. This refers to the five aggregates, consisting of forms, feelings, discriminations, compositional factors, and the six kinds of consciousness, which together constitute body and mind. These undergo change moment by moment. Since the person is attributed to these five aggregates, the world in this context alludes primarily to the person. The whole recurrent process of involuntary birth and death, of one rebirth after another in the six realms of existence, is also referred to as the world. And the woes of the world, particularly our human woes, are birth, aging, sickness, death, not getting what we want, experiencing what we do not want, and seeking but not finding what we desire, as well as the many other troubles we face.

These unwanted miseries come from ignorance, and only through understanding the profound nature of dependent arising can we stop the suffering, the compulsive actions, the disturbing emotions, and the misconceptions which lie at their root. In their works the great Indian masters Aryadeva, Buddhapalita, Chandrakirti, and Shantideva[8] stress that the Buddha and Nagarjuna conclusively stated that the correct understanding of reality is essential not only for the attainment of highest enlightenment but also for attaining the state of Foe Destroyer in the Hearer and Solitary Realizer vehicles.[9] Whatever effort we make to gain this knowledge is not to please the Buddha or our spiritual teachers but for our own great benefit. To equip ourselves for this quest, we need a spiritual teacher who has a good knowledge of the subject and is willing to communicate that knowledge. We need access to the great classical texts which explain the nature of reality, and we need plenty of enthusiasm.

When we begin to explore the nature of reality, it is not really productive to look outwards at externally existent things. Our search will be more fruitful if we turn our attention inwards to scrutinize our own condition and mode of existence. When we have understood that, it will be relatively easy to understand the rest. Once we have seen reality as it is, nothing anyone else says can rob us of that understanding because it will be based on confident conviction.

THE PERFECTION OF
WISDOM SUTRAS

There is much debate regarding what constitutes the Buddha's word.[10] The different schools of Buddhist philosophy[11] put forward a variety of views. The Vaibhashikas assert that the Buddha's word consists of a collection of names, words, and syllables and that this collection is a non-associated compositional factor.[12] According to the Sautrantikas the Buddha's word is an external form and the object of auditory consciousness. The Prasangika view accords with common perception that the word of the Buddha is sound and physical matter. Physical forms are an aggregation of particles, of which the smallest are difficult to identify and mistakenly thought by some to be permanent entities, that is, not undergoing momentary change. A certain duration of time, such as a year, can be broken down into months, weeks, days, hours, minutes, and seconds, and again the very smallest components of time are considered by some to be permanent.[13] When language is similarly broken down, the smallest components are syllables, which certain Indian non-Buddhist schools of philosophy assert are permanent. This indicates the difficulties involved in ascertaining how things actually exist.

The Chittamatrin view is that if the Buddha's word were actual sound, then the words the Buddha spoke could not have existed in his mind before being spoken. They assert that Buddhahood or enlightenment is posited in relation to the exalted wisdom which directly perceives and knows all phenomena and which constantly remains in meditative equipoise on their fundamental nature. Through the perfect prayers of aspiration to help living beings that a Buddha has made and through the presence of students whose karma is pure and whose mindstreams are mature and receptive, the enjoyment body of an enlightened being appears to teach exalted Bodhisattvas and the emanation body to teach Hearers, Solitary Realizers, and others.[14] The Buddha's word is this appearance of teaching.

Whichever way it is defined, the Buddha's word consists of sutras which were spoken by the Buddha himself and sutras inspired by him, which were spoken by others through his blessings. The Perfection of Wisdom sutras contain both these forms of his teaching.

These sutras were taught on Vulture's Peak outside Rajgir. The Tibetan name for this place literally means the vulture's (or vultures') heap (or pile) mountain.[15] There are different ideas regarding why it was known by this name. Some say it was shaped like a vulture or like a vulture's head or that vultures used to congregate there. It is also said that many exalted Bodhisattvas with direct perception of emptiness came in the form of vultures from other worlds to hear the Enlightened One teach. When we go to teachings, we like to have a good seat and we try to impress others by being as grand as possible or sitting very still and straight. But Bodhisattvas appear in any form that they consider appropriate and are not concerned with such matters!

Before the Buddha taught he touched the ground, just as he did in Bodhgaya,[16] and it became hard as a diamond, indestructible by fire, and such that intermediate state beings, who can normally pass through solid matter, could not pass through it. He adorned the place where he would teach and prepared his own seat, to which he paid homage as a symbol of his respect for the teaching he was about to give. It is said that he gave this teaching one year after his enlightenment.

The different versions of the Perfection of Wisdom sutras are sometimes referred to as the six "mothers" and the eleven "children." However, the best known are the long version consisting of a hundred thousand verses, the middling version of twenty-five thousand verses, and the short one of eight thousand verses.[17] On one occasion when His Holiness the Dalai Lama visited Vulture's Peak, he read the *Perfection of Wisdom Sutra in Eight Thousand Verses* there. This is a clear indication of his reverence for these sutras.

It has been the custom of Tibetan scholars to recite the classical texts by great Indian and Tibetan masters when on pilgrimage to Buddhist holy places in India. In Bodhgaya Maitreya's *Ornament for Clear Realization*,[18] Vasubandhu's *Treasury of Knowledge*[19] or Chandrakirti's *Supplement to the Middle Way*[20] are traditionally recited. The *Heart Sutra* is often recited at Vulture's Peak and Je Tsongkhapa's *Praise for Dependent Arising* in the former great seat of learning, Nalanda.[21] I remember that when His Holiness the Dalai Lama travelled to the site of the monastic university of Nalanda with his two tutors, Kyabje Ling Rinpoche and Kyabje Trijang Rinpoche,[22] the tutors staged a debate there to commemorate and honor the illustrious scholars of ancient India, who lived in that monastery during the centuries when Nalanda flourished.

According to the Tibetan tradition, five sutras are famed for containing different forms of a hundred thousand: the longest of the Perfection of Wisdom sutras has one hundred thousand verses and is called the hundred thousand of the mind. The *State Beyond Sorrow Sutra* contains one hundred thousand last instructions, which the Enlightened One gave before passing away, and is called the hundred thousand of the speech. The *Heap of Jewels Sutra* contains the names of a hundred thousand Buddhas and is known as the hundred thousand of the body. The *Buddha Avatamsaka Sutra* contains a hundred thousand prayers of aspiration and is known as the hundred thousand of good qualities, and the *Descent into Lanka Sutra*, which contains the methods for taming one hundred thousand ogres, is the hundred thousand of enlightened activity.[23]

Each of these sutras has a shorter form which condenses its contents. These shorter forms are the *Heart Sutra*, the *Wisdom on Passing Beyond Sorrow*, the *Adamantine Destroyer of All*, the *Prayer of Noble Conduct*, and the *Confession Sutra*.[24] These five sutras respectively deal with the correct view; conduct; ablution ceremonies for removing impurities, obstacles, and interferences; prayers of aspiration; and the purification of wrong-doing. They became known as the "sutras of the kings" because the great religious kings of Tibet recited these short sutras themselves and made them popular.

It is said that the Perfection of Wisdom sutras reached Tibet during the reign of Trisong Detsen, when a certain Langkhampa Gocha, who had perfect recall of anything he committed to memory, was sent to India to bring back these sutras.[25] He memorized the *Perfection of Wisdom Sutra in One Hundred Thousand Verses* and the story goes that on his return, when he came into the king's presence, he was dressed as a traditional Tibetan scripture, which contains loose folios between endboards. On his back he wore a golden board and on his front a turquoise one. Wrapped around his middle to keep them in place was a string of pearls. All this was intended to denote the preciousness of what he had brought back to Tibet. The sutra was then written down in ink made from the king's blood mixed with precious jewels that had been ground down. In the past benefactors donated gold and jewels for the writing of sacred texts, and some versions of the Buddha's speech were written in gold so thick that you could easily scratch some off with your fingernail.

We should not feel incredulous about Langkhampa's powers of memory. The Kadampa master Geshe Sharawa[26] knew the hundred and eight volumes of the Buddha's word by heart, and even in my time I have known masters who had perfectly memorized the five works of Maitreya or Je Tsongkhapa's *Great Exposition of the Stages of the Path.*[27]

THE HEART SUTRA

According to Tibetan tradition, there is a custom of reciting certain verses before one begins to teach or to read the sutras and other texts aloud. For example, His Holiness the Dalai Lama and other great teachers frequently recite the following verse from the *King of Prayers*:

> In the languages of god, nagas,[28] and harmful spirits,
> In those of ghouls and human beings,
> In as many tones as living creatures utter,
> In all of these will I give teachings.

These words express the strong wish that not only humans but other living creatures may hear and benefit from what is said, and one imagines teaching them as well as those who are actually before one.

In Tibet we used to go out into the mountain meadows and play the flute. We did this in spring when everything begins to grow, when animals come out of hibernation and other creatures living deep in the ground come up to the surface. We thought of the music bringing pleasure not only to humans but to these other living beings as well. We never played the flute this way when the ground grew hard with the onset of winter, in case the music might lure these creatures from their burrows and from the earth and cause them suffering instead of delight. Similarly, we used to go into the mountains and chant the mantra *Om Mani Padme Hung*[29] very loudly so that all the creatures around might hear it and benefit. These customs were based on a sense of compassion that was part of our culture.

In the great monastic universities in Tibet recitations of the *Heart Sutra* were often preceded by this verse:

> Homage to the mother of the Victors of the three times—
> To the perfection of wisdom beyond thought
> and expression,
> Unborn, unceasing, in the nature of space,
> The object of the exalted wisdom which knows itself.

It is said these words were spoken by the Buddha's son Rahula in praise of his mother. It seems, however, not to be his mother in the normal sense but the perfection of wisdom, which is also referred to as the mother. The meaning of the verse is that both the direct perception of emptiness which liberates us from cyclic existence and the direct perception of emptiness possessed by those who are liberated from cyclic existence cannot be described as it actually is by language nor understood conceptually. It is not produced in terms of inherent existence and thus also does not cease inherently. For this reason its final mode of existence is the mere negation of inherent existence in the same way that space is a mere negation or absence of obstructive form. This wisdom is the mother of the enlightened ones of the past, present and future. The term "mother" is used of emptiness itself, of the understanding of emptiness and of the Perfection of Wisdom sutras, which explain that understanding and the nature of emptiness. In ancient India the father was said to determine the specific caste, such as the royal caste or warrior caste, and the family to which a child belonged. Similarly, great compassion, love, the spirit of enlightenment[30] and so forth are the specific qualities pertaining to the skillful means aspect of practice which determine whether or not one belongs to the Mahayana vehicle. Just as a mother gives birth to children irrespective of the caste to which they belong, so the understanding of emptiness gives rise to the exalted ones of the Hearer, Solitary Realizer, and Mahayana vehicles and to exalted Buddhas. Maitreya's *Sublime Continuum* says:

> The aspiration for [the enlightenment of] the supreme vehicle is the [father's] seed. Wisdom is the mother that gives birth to Buddhahood.[31]

In the Indian language: *Bhagavatīprajñāpāramitāhṛdaya*
In the Tibetan language: *bCom ldan 'das ma shes rab kyi pha rol tu phyin pa'i snying po*
[In the English language: *The Essence of the Perfection of Wisdom, the Victorious*]

One section

Homage to the Perfection of Wisdom, the Victorious.[32]

The title stands first for the purpose of identifying a sutra or text. The Tibetan *nyingpo* (*snying po*) is the essence and is connected with the word *nying* (*snying*), meaning heart. Although consciousness pervades the body, its principal seat is the heart center, which is where the consciousness is located when the embryo first forms. As the fetus grows, awareness gradually expands and extends. At death once more consciousness withdraws into the heart center, so one could say this is where the essence of consciousness resides. Similarly, the whole meaning of the Perfection of Wisdom sutras is condensed within the *Heart Sutra* or more correctly the *Essence* or *Heart of the Perfection of Wisdom*, which expresses the Buddha's underlying thought and intention in the most concise form. As Je Tsongkhapa says in his *Praise for Dependent Arising*:

> All that you taught both starts from and
> Proceeds to relativity
> Alone. Nirvana being the goal
> No deed of yours was not for peace.

The Buddha's sole purpose was to help living beings, without making any distinctions between them, to free themselves from suffering and reach the supreme state of happiness, referred to as non-abiding nirvana.[33] Everything he taught was intended to lead to the understanding of emptiness, which enables us to attain freedom.

What reaches nirvana? The reality of our minds which is known as the essence of those who have gone to bliss.[34] Our minds have a conventional nature and an ultimate nature. The conventional nature of the mind, which is its clarity and cognizance, is not affected by the disturbing emotions and misconceptions, since these temporary stains are not an integral part of the mind. This is self-evident because we are not constantly angry or constantly desirous. These emotions arise only when certain circumstances come together. It is therefore possible to free our minds from them if we apply the appropriate antidotes. Only the understanding of emptiness has the power to uproot the disturbing emotions completely, which is why it acts as the ultimate antidote. Other antidotes have a temporary effect, in that they prevent the disturbing emotions from arising or from continuing once they have arisen.

The emptiness of the mind is referred to as natural nirvana[35]—natural because the mind, like all else that exists, has from the very outset always been free from true or inherent existence. This is why the mental stains, which are temporary, can be removed and why we can attain liberation. In general, according to the Prasangika school, both nirvana and true cessation are ultimate truths and emptiness.[36] However, there are certain masters, such as Panchen Sönam Drakpa,[37] who hold that both nirvana and true cessation are ultimate truths but not emptiness because emptiness is the negation of true or inherent existence, which is something totally non-existent. According to them true cessation and nirvana, on the other hand, are the preclusion of or separation from something existent, namely the disturbing emotions, misconceptions, and so forth, of which we need to rid ourselves.

The reality of the mind with stains will one day be the nature body of an enlightened being, namely the emptiness of an enlightened being's mind, while the mind with stains will become the wisdom truth body of an enlightened being. From the Prasangika point of view we all have the potential for this, which is referred to as Buddha nature.

The term Buddha nature, when translated literally from Tibetan, means the lineage or disposition for Buddhahood. The Vaibhashika and Sautrantika schools do not speak of Buddha nature but of the disposition of the exalted which has four features: contentment with simple clothes, which in the case of ordained people means their three basic robes; contentment with a simple mattress, in other words with basic living conditions; contentment with simple food and drink, such as living on alms where ordained people are concerned; and having a liking for eliminating what needs to be overcome and for meditation.[38] The first two noble truths—true suffering and true sources of suffering—are what we must overcome and to do this we must accomplish the true paths of insight through meditation.

Having adopted such a simple lifestyle, we may encounter

difficulties in obtaining food, clothing, and shelter. Instead of allowing this to discourage us, we should instead view these difficulties as a result of our own past actions. If we have a strong resolve never to give up this way of life, we will be able to observe ethical discipline, which is fundamental to the practice of the Buddha's teachings. We will please the enlightened ones and their children, the Bodhisattvas, and thereby experience their blessings.

This is useful advice about cultivating contentment and having few wishes. Our greed to acquire this and that and our lack of contentment with what we have—wanting more or what is better—give us so much trouble. By cultivating contentment, limiting our desires, and practicing meditation in the proper way, we can ourselves become exalted beings and gain liberation.

The Chittamatrins consist of the followers of scripture and the followers of reasoning.[39] The former assert the existence of the foundational consciousness and that it bears the seeds of uncontaminated mind.[40] While the seeds are latent they are the innately abiding disposition and when they are activated through hearing the teachings and thinking about them, they become the developmental disposition.[41] The followers of reasoning assert the same but say that the seeds are carried within mental consciousness.

The Prasangika Madhyamika school defines the innately abiding disposition as the reality of the mind with stains, which acts as its basis, being that which can become the nature body of an enlightened being. They define the developmental disposition as a produced phenomenon which can become the other bodies of an enlightened being.[42] This refers to the wisdom truth body and the two kinds of form bodies.

Once we realize that everything the Buddha taught was intended to lead us to the understanding of emptiness, which is the mother of the Buddhas of the three times, we will recognize that there are no contradictions in the teachings and that, instead, they reveal the Buddha's consummate skill in guiding those with very different abilities and interests.

After the title we find the words "One section." There is no standard number of verses which constitute a "section," and different sutras have sections of differing lengths. The number of sections for different categories of sutras was determined by the translators. In the *Heart Sutra* the number of verses is twenty-five, a number also found in other sutras.[43] The translator specified the number of sections to insure that nothing would subsequently be added to or deleted from the original text.

This is followed by the translator's homage made to create the auspicious circumstances for the completion of his work. He pays homage to the perfection of wisdom. In Tibetan the words that are here translated as "perfection of wisdom" literally mean the wisdom gone beyond.[44] There are different ways in which certain things are beyond others. For instance, exalted beings are beyond or transcend ordinary beings, ultimate reality transcends conventional reality, the state beyond sorrow transcends cyclic existence, and the understanding of reality transcends confusion.

For Chittamatrins the perfection of wisdom is only the perfected understanding that what is perceived and the perceiving awareness are not separate entities,[45] and for Svatantrikas, too, the perfection of wisdom only refers to omniscient mind[46] itself. According to them, the paths of insight that lead to this perfection and the texts which reveal how to cultivate this understanding are simply called the perfection of wisdom but are not the actual perfection. Only an omniscient mind, which has transcended the obstructions to knowledge of all phenomena, can fully understand the varying capacities and dispositions of students and thus know the most effective ways of leading individuals out of confusion. The Prasangikas, however, consider both the perfected understanding and the understanding of one who is still training as the perfection of wisdom.

THE PROLOGUE

Thus I have heard. At one time the Victor was at Vulture's Peak near Rajgir together with a great assembly of the fully ordained and a great assembly of Bodhisattvas.

The prologue has a general and a specific part. Its purpose is to inspire us to take good note of what is said in the main part of the sutra by reassuring us that the one who compiled this sutra was actually present and able fully to retain what was taught.

The general part of the prologue supplies information regarding the location and the audience. It reveals that this teaching and the circumstances under which it was given were distinguished by four kinds of excellence. The teaching was given at an excellent time by an excellent teacher in an excellent place in the presence of an excellent audience. The time was excellent because it was while the Buddha Shakyamuni was alive. The words "At one time" have been interpreted in different ways.

The Indian master Haribhadra[47] says that Ananda,[48] the compiler of this sutra, heard and understood the whole teaching on the perfection of wisdom in a single moment. The Indian master Bhavaviveka[49] states that Ananda, being a practitioner of the Hearer Vehicle, could not have understood the Buddha's teaching on the perfection of wisdom properly and that, therefore, the Perfection of Wisdom sutras were compiled by Vajrapani and other Bodhisattvas.[50] Haribhadra, however, asserts that though Ananda could not have comprehended this subject-matter fully of his own accord, he was able to do so through the Buddha's blessings.

Although it may seem difficult to imagine that Ananda could have heard and understood it all in a single instant, through the blessings of an enlightened one, what usually takes a long time can occur in an instant and what normally takes an instant can happen over an extended period. Ananda's task was not easy. He had to hear nothing more nor less than what was said. He had to understand it, remember it, and then recite it from memory.

The excellent teacher was the Buddha Shakyamuni, the Enlightened One himself. The excellent place was Vulture's Peak outside Rajgir, as has already been explained. Rajgir was a flourishing town and is thus associated with secular activities and the afflicted side of things. It is said that King Bimbisara[51] originally lived in Kushinagar.[52] A particular part of the town burned down repeatedly due to the nefarious activities of certain spirits. The king decreed that the next family whose house burned down would have to build their home in the charnel ground of Sitavana. As it happened the king's palace caught fire and so it was he who had to move first. The place where he rebuilt his palace became known as Rajagriha, the house of the king, and it became the royal seat. This account is found in the *Rice Seedling Sutra*.[53] The town is in the modern Indian state of Bihar and is now called Rajgir.[54] Vulture's Peak is some way outside Rajgir, removed from the world of secular activities. It is associated with the spiritual and thus with the purified side of things.

The excellent audience of those present consists of a great assembly of the fully ordained and a great assembly of Bodhisattvas. There are ten ways of becoming fully ordained. In this context the fully ordained are Foe Destroyers, namely those who have freed themselves from the disturbing emotions and their seeds, our true foes, and thus from cyclic existence. Observance of some form of the individual liberation vow,[55] of which the vow of a fully ordained monk or nun is supreme, is the foundation for the flourishing of the Buddha's teaching, and Foe Destroyers observe that ethical discipline in the most perfect way. Through the Buddha's teachings many became Foe Destroyers during his lifetime. Mahakashyapa[56] and other Foe Destroyers acted as compilers of the Buddha's teachings and in this way, too, were the foundation for their flourishing. It is said that sixteen Foe Destroyers[57] are still in different places, protecting the teachings and thereby also helping them to flourish.

The Tibetan word *gendun* (*dge bdun*) has been translated as "assembly" here and is often translated as "the spiritual community," but it literally means aspirants to virtue.[58] Such an assembly consists of four or more fully ordained people and comes into being when the aspiration is present not to be separated through any demonic force from the teacher, the scriptural teachings, the teachings in the form of insights, or from spiritual companions.

Also present was a great assembly of Bodhisattvas. The Tibetan for Bodhisattva is *jangchup sempa* (*byang chub sems dpa'*). *Jangchup* refers to the state of enlightenment in which one has completely purified (*jang*) all faults and limitations and has perfected all understanding (*chup*), good qualities, and insights. Here it is extended to include Bodhisattvas who have already purified a great many faults and developed considerable qualities and insights. The first syllable of *sempa* means mind and the second means hero. A Bodhisattva again and again takes to mind the welfare of living beings and has the heroic ability to overcome interferences and everything hostile.

According to another interpretation of *jangchup sempa, jang* refers to training in and *chup* to fully understanding the two truths. A Bodhisattva is one who heroically faces and bears the hardship of contemplating the two truths again and again.

A great assembly refers to a large number and in the case of the Bodhisattvas mentioned, they are, moreover, endowed with six kinds of greatness. They are greatly generous in that they are willing to give away their body, possessions, and virtue. They gladly give to those in need and enjoy the immediate pleasure of having satisfied another's wishes as well as the long-term benefits that result from generosity.

They are greatly intelligent, being capable of comprehending the intricacies of conventional phenomena and of understanding the fundamental nature of things. They are greatly powerful with the capacity to overcome everything inimical. They are greatly engaged in Mahayana practices, which consist of taking responsibility for others' well-being, in contrast to Hinayana practices, where the focus is limited to responsibility for oneself and one's own liberation. They are greatly armored with patience and enthusiastic effort. When harmed they do not think of retaliating but instead feel even stronger compassion and the wish to insure the happiness of the one who has harmed them. They are great tamers of all destructive forces.

The word "together" in the phrase "together with a great assembly" indicates that all those present were harmoniously engaged in the same activity and there was no dissension.

On that occasion the Victor was absorbed in a concentration on the diversity of phenomena called "profound appearance." Also at that time the Bodhisattva, that great being, the exalted and powerful Avalokiteshvara was contemplating the profound practice of the perfection of wisdom, and he saw that the five aggregates, too, are empty of any inherent nature.

Now we begin the part of the prologue which describes the particular circumstances. "On that occasion" indicates that the minds of those gathered at Vulture's Peak were mature through the ripening of imprints from the past and receptive to the teaching they were about to hear. The Buddha was in meditative equipoise and would soon inspire and bless Shariputra and Avalokiteshvara[59] for the sake of all those who were present and ready.

"Profound appearance" refers to perception of the fundamental way in which things exist, which is hard to take to mind and understand. A lake can easily encompass the reflection of the sun or moon but cannot reflect the whole sky. Conventional matters are easy to take to mind but not ultimate reality, about which we can only think with difficulty. "Appearance" here refers to the way in which the object appears to direct perception with total clarity and without obstruction. The Buddha is not meditating on the multiplicity of phenomena but perceiving the emptiness, the fundamental mode of existence, of as many phenomena as there are. Everything that exists can be included within the aggregates, sources, and constituents,[60] whose reality he is contemplating.

The Buddha will bless Avalokiteshvara when he has fully understood what is necessary and is ready to give instruction. Avalokiteshvara is called exalted[61] because this distinguishes him from ordinary beings. The latter may be very ordinary like most of us or may already be considerably accomplished like Bodhisattvas on the paths of accumulation and preparation.[62] It is only when the four phases—heat, peak, patience, and supreme qualities— of the path of preparation have been traversed and the path of seeing is reached that one becomes an exalted being. Avalokiteshvara watches over all living beings with the wish to free them from suffering. He is powerful because he has control over that wish and is completely ruled by compassion. Through the power of the Buddha, who is absorbed in concentration, Avalokiteshvara has been engaged in hearing and thinking about the resultant perfection of wisdom, the path perfection of wisdom and the scriptural perfection of wisdom.

In the teachings we often come across the terms hearing, thinking, and meditating used together. Hearing comprises hearing the spoken word but also reading the written word and recalling what has been heard or read. During his contemplation Avalokiteshvara understands that the five aggregates are merely posited by naming and do not have any intrinsic existence from their own side. The word "too" in "he saw that the five aggregates, too, are empty of any inherent nature" means he understands that not only do the aggregates exist in this way but also the sources and constituents.

The fact that Avalokiteshvara understands this as a result of the Buddha's blessing and that he then passes on to others what he has understood indicates the importance of receiving teachings which have come down to us as part of a living lineage.

THE QUESTION

Then, through the power of the Buddha, the venerable Shariputra asked the Bodhisattva, that great being, the exalted and powerful Avalokiteshvara, "How should any child of the noble lineage who wants to perform the profound activity of perfecting wisdom proceed?"

The dialogue only begins when the Buddha is satisfied that Avalokiteshvara has fully understood what he will communicate. This shows that a teacher should have a sound understanding of what he or she teaches. The student will feel confident if the teacher has a thorough command of the material. Without this neither is on firm ground. It is useless to hope for results, such as insights and greater control of the mind, unless we create the corresponding causes. If we have a real interest in the teachings, we will want to experience the results they can bring. This will only happen when we do what accords with the teachings, which describe to us the attainment, how to accomplish it, and what we need to do in preparation. Je Tsongkhapa points out that it is a mistake to think that the sutras, tantras, and the great commentaries are to be studied for intellectual knowledge and that when it comes to practice, we need to look elsewhere for instruction.

To receive the blessings which make our mindstreams serviceable, we imagine our spiritual teacher in the form of the Buddha or of a meditational deity. We then request this teacher and the other teachers of the spiritual lineage to bless us and make us receptive. This is like preparing the field for the seed. If we sow it when the field has been ploughed and prepared and the temperature is right, seedlings will soon appear. Similarly, when the warmth of these blessings is in our mindstreams and we sow the seeds of hearing and thinking, insights will grow.

When I first entered Sera Monastery in Tibet, Geshe Lhudrup Thapkey[63] was the abbot. He used to ride to Norbu Lingka[64] from Sera on horseback, and I remember hearing that during this journey he could recite by heart the whole of Je Tsongkhapa's great text the *Essence of Eloquence*[65] on the philosophical tenets of the different schools. He was one of the scholars who later accompanied His Holiness the Dalai Lama when he traveled to China in 1954. When these great masters came to the debating court everyone would fall silent and listen with bated breath to their debate. They continued to recite the texts with which they felt the closest affinity long after they became fully qualified teachers because they found that as they did so, their understanding grew more and more profound. Although we may never manage to learn the whole of the *Essence of Eloquence*, we can learn the *Heart Sutra* and recite it not merely parrot-fashion but with some understanding of the philosophical view it expounds.

For whose benefit did the Buddha inspire the dialogue between Shariputra and Avalokiteshvara? For those present on that occasion and for us. Buddhas are always ready to act when the student's mindstream is sufficiently open and mature. This doesn't mean that they have to rush from place to place. They can rest in meditative equipoise while acting for our benefit.

Shariputra, who asks the question, is given the title *venerable* but in fact the Tibetan words are *tse dang denpa* (*tshe dang ldan pa*), which means having life. This title was normally used when speaking about or addressing a junior monk, just as the term *nayten* (*gnas brtan*), meaning something like firm in his place, was used for an elder or senior monk. However, since Ananda, the compiler of the sutra, was junior to Shariputra, the words here have a different meaning, namely having a life free from the disturbing emotions and from the bonds of contaminated action driven by these emotions. In Tibet, as in India, using the correct forms of address and respect for senior monks was an important part of monastic discipline.

Why does Shariputra need to ask this question if he is liberated from cyclic existence? Even though he is a Foe Destroyer, it does not necessarily follow that he fully understands everything the Buddha taught in the Perfection of Wisdom sutras. He could be asking the question in order to receive transmission of these instructions because, as has been noted, to hold the living lineage has always been considered vital among the followers of the Buddha. He may also be asking the question for the sake of the others present.

Shariputra's mother was called Sharika because she had eyes like a *sharika*, a bird living in the reed forests. His name means son of Shari. He is said to have been an emanation of one of the eight Bodhisattvas closest to the Buddha, Sarvanivarana Vishkambhin, whose name means the one who removes obstructions.

Children of the noble lineage are those whose Mahayana disposition[66] has awakened and who have developed the spirit of enlightenment. The word "any" in "How should any child of the noble lineage..." implies those who have a strong interest in discovering the nature of reality and who are not afraid of emptiness. It is possible to make the mistake of thinking lack of inherent existence means non-existence. It is also possible to reject the idea that things lack inherent existence on the grounds that we can see and feel them. Both of these are very real dangers.

The following words from the sutra act as a transition from the question to the answer and then, initially, present the answer in a concise form.

The Bodhisattva, that great being, the exalted and powerful Avalokiteshvara answered the venerable Shariputra, saying,

"Any sons or daughters of the noble lineage who want to perform the profound activity of perfecting wisdom should consider things in the following way. They should clearly see that the five aggregates also are empty of any inherent nature.

From "The Bodhisattva..." to "...in the following way" is the transition. Avalokiteshvara's first brief and then extensive answers use many words to show those with duller faculties how to practice. For those with the sharpest faculties the mantra, which contains the full instructions, is enough.

Avalokiteshvara speaks of sons and daughters of the noble lineage. This indicates that those who are distinctly men or women can understand and practice the perfection of wisdom, not those whose gender is unclear, such as eunuchs or hermaphrodites. This is not said out of prejudice but because their condition is likely to make their minds unstable. If it is so difficult for those with a mind more stable than our own to gain these insights, how much more difficult would it be for those with an even less stable mind?

"They should clearly see that the five aggregates also are empty of any inherent nature" is the concise answer. Avalokiteshvara states that we need to understand that the five aggregates—forms, feelings, discriminations, compositional factors, and consciousnesses—are empty of inherent existence because they are all products dependent upon causes and conditions and upon their parts. Contemplation of this is meditation.

On the path of accumulation one engages with the perfection of wisdom through deriving the knowledge gained from hearing and thinking. The practice consists mainly of analytical meditation. According to Tendar Lharampa's[67] commentary the concise answer directly indicates what is done on the path of accumulation and indirectly indicates what is done on the path of preparation. The longer answer, which follows, directly shows how to practice on the path of preparation, where one gains the knowledge derived from meditation through alternating analytical and placement meditation.

The word "also" in "the five aggregates also..." indicates that not only the I lacks any inherent existence but also what is mine. One begins by meditating on the selflessness of the person, which comprises the selflessness of the I and mine. When the selflessness of the I has been well understood, one will easily understand the selflessness of mine, just as when a chariot is burned, its parts are burned as well.

The great masters advise us to begin by meditating on the selflessness of the person rather than on the selflessness of other phenomena. In both cases what is negated is exactly the same, namely inherent existence. But because we can only think of the person or self in relation to body and mind, it is easier to recognize the person's lack of independent or inherent existence. Similarly, phenomena that are conventionally accepted as deceptive, such as an echo, a mirage of water, a dream, or the reflection of the face in the mirror, and those that are not considered deceptive, such as the body or mind, all lack intrinsic existence in exactly the same way, but it is easier to see the emptiness of those things that are normally considered deceptive. This is because on a more superficial level we already know that they are not as they appear. These deceptive phenomena serve as a useful gateway to the understanding of emptiness.

Lack of inherent existence means that something does not exist objectively, from its own side, in and of itself. Our dreaming mind creates the elephant that appears in our dream. That dream elephant doesn't appear from its own side. In the same way, all conventional phenomena are posited merely by force of appearing to the mind and there is nothing existent that is not posited in this way. For Prasangikas the object of refutation by reasoning is inherent existence and therefore the *Heart Sutra* is for them a definitive sutra, whose meaning can be taken literally. For other schools of Buddhist philosophy, such as the Svatantrika school, if things did not have inherent existence, they would be totally non-existent and so they qualify what is said by asserting that they have no *ultimate* inherent existence, since they do not have any ultimate existence. Thus for them the *Heart Sutra* is interpretable.[68]

FORM IS EMPTY

Form is empty. Emptiness is form. Emptiness is not other than form and form is not other than emptiness. Similarly, feelings, discriminations, compositional factors, and consciousnesses are also empty.

According to Tendar Lharampa's commentary, this part of the answer primarily indicates how one practices on the path of preparation. The profound is now explained in terms of four attributes. Of the five aggregates, form is the first. Form exists in dependence upon a basis of attribution and the process of attribution by terms and concepts. It thus is empty of any existence from its own side. Not the smallest part of any form is inherently existent. Its nature is therefore emptiness.

If we accept this form, which is merely attributed by thought and naming, as it appears and make no investigation, it operates in a satisfactory way and exists—as a mere appearance. It functions and is therefore not at all non-existent. Form thus has two aspects or identities: its conventional nature and its ultimate nature. In his *Supplement to the Middle Way,* Chandrakirti says:

> Since the correct and false are seen in all things,
> Things in their diversity have two identities.

What is the relationship between the conventional nature and the ultimate nature of a thing? They are like water and wetness, a white conch shell and its white color, fire and heat, or like that which is made or produced and impermanence. For instance, water and wetness are different but they are one entity, in that you cannot have the one without the other. Similarly, the emptiness of an object and the object itself are one entity. If the emptiness of form were a different entity from form itself, it would follow that form should be truly existent. "Emptiness is no other than form" because emptiness and form are not different entities but one entity. The two can be named and thought of separately but the one cannot exist without the other.

If a form were inherently existent, it couldn't depend on causes and conditions and thus would be a causeless result. Although they are not cause and effect, emptiness and form have a somewhat similar relationship because we say that things are empty of intrinsic existence because they depend on causes and conditions, upon parts, and upon the process of attribution. Because they are empty of intrinsic existence they can appear, are conventionally existent, and function satisfactorily.

There are different ways in which something can be absent. The absence of yoghurt at the time of the milk which will be used to make it is absence at a previous time. The absence of milk when the yoghurt has been made is absence through disintegration. The absence of a pot in a place where there is no bulbous thing is the absence of non-existence. The absence of a horse in an ox is the absence of one thing in another. The absence of a human, when one mistakes a scarecrow for a person, is the absence of that entity or identity. The latter is the kind of absence which is referred to when we say that form is empty of inherent existence.

From the Prasangika point of view the different terms like empty of inherent existence, intrinsic existence, true existence, objective existence, existence from its own side, and existence in and of itself all have the same meaning, while other schools make a difference between, for instance, true and inherent existence. What need is there to use such a variety of terms if according to the Prasangikas they all have the same meaning? Firstly because the other schools make distinctions between them but also because a particular term will evoke the meaning vividly and make a profound impact on one individual, while another will not. In the same way many analogies, such as mirages, dreams, echoes, magicians' illusions, and reflections, are employed to illustrate that things are not truly existent as they appear to be. Different people will feel an affinity with different analogies. The one that we feel drawn to may have the power to unlock a deeper understanding. We can say "things are empty of inherent existence" till the cows come home, but if we do not understand what empty implies in this context and what it would be like for something to be inherently existent, the words will not have much meaning for us.

Thus form is empty of inherent existence and that emptiness is the ultimate nature of the form which exists and functions conventionally. Its emptiness is not inherently different from form and form is not a different entity from its emptiness of inherent existence. This illustrates how to meditate on the profound in terms of four attributes.

Why are they presented here in relation to the first aggregate, that of form? When contemplating the emptiness of the aggregates, it is most useful to turn our attention to our own body and mind. Our physical form is like a container, while the other four aggregates, which are all different aspects of awareness, are like the contents. When the container breaks, the contents, which have nowhere to stay, disperse. When we understand the emptiness of form, we will with relative ease be able to understand the emptiness of the other aggregates—feelings, discriminations, compositional factors consisting of all the other mental functions, and the different kinds of consciousness.

We ordinary people are greatly preoccupied with forms of every kind and our attachment to them keeps us in cyclic existence. Through understanding their emptiness we can liberate ourselves. At present our clinging and craving are constantly stimulated. This feels exhilarating and pleasurable at the beginning, but when the craving intensifies it becomes painful and makes us restless. In that state of intense stimulation all we can think about is "How am I going to get it?" To us the sense objects appear thoroughly existent from their own side and this is why we respond to them in the way we do.

The extent to which we are fascinated by form is easily seen when we regard our own interests and those of the people around us. Sights, sounds, smells, tastes, and tactile sensations dominate our lives and are of consuming interest to us. We consider design important and are particular about the shape and color of the things we wear and have in our home, so much so that we are prepared to invest much time and energy in finding exactly what we want. We enjoy fragrances both natural and artificial and pay a lot of money to buy perfumes, room sprays, fragrant candles, potpourri mixtures, and the like. Food, of course, plays a major role in all our lives and chefs go to great lengths to create new dishes to stimulate jaded palates. The many new textiles that are invented are not just to create a new look but promise new and agreeable tactile sensations for the wearer— comfortable fabrics that breathe and stretch. This is the stuff of our daily lives and many people hardly think beyond these matters.

The appearance, sound, smell, taste, and sensation of another person are even more compelling than the external sense objects, namely those not linked to the consciousness of a living being. Our addiction to tastes of different kinds is responsible for many health problems and our craving for the tactile sensations involved in sexual activity easily leads to disease and conflict, thereby endangering our lives.

Ignorance gives rise to actions which leave imprints on our mindstreams. These imprints are triggered by craving and grasping and produce further rebirth in cyclic existence. It is therefore apt to say that attachment or craving is responsible for our continued cyclic existence. Thinking about the fact that form is empty helps break our habit of reifying the objects of the senses and the feelings we experience in relation to them.

The statement that emptiness is form counteracts the opposite tendency to underestimate the status of things, which leads to the extreme of nihilism. For this reason the existence of form and its ability to function, although it is empty of inherent existence, is stressed. Emptiness may be seen as an escape route into a state of detachment and personal peace, but emptiness and appearance must be given equal value and importance. In order to prevent us from falling into such a state, which can result from intensive meditation on emptiness, the dependently existent nature of things is stressed. This reminds us to pay attention to the development of skillful means, because contemplating the way we and others remain imprisoned in cyclic existence will stimulate our compassion for them and make us wish to help them find relief from suffering. The dependently existent nature of things also makes us recall the connection between actions and their effects and how we and others are in this painful condition because of our past actions.

Finding the middle way is rather like walking on a path between an abyss and barbed wire. If we step too far in the one direction to avoid the barbed wire, we plummet into the abyss of nihilism. If to avoid this danger we move too far to the other side, we get caught in the extreme of permanence or reification. The Buddha showed us how to avoid these two extremes by following the middle way.

THE EIGHT ASPECTS

In all three vehicles—the Hearer, Solitary Realizer, and Great vehicles—there are five paths. On the third of these, the path of seeing, the meditator overcomes intellectually formed misconceptions apprehending the signs of true existence in external and internal phenomena by developing the exalted direct understanding that the sphere of phenomena, emptiness, is present in all things. To gain this realization the meditator contemplates eight aspects which can be subsumed under the three doors to liberation.[69]

The *Heart Sutra* says:

Likewise, Shariputra, all phenomena are empty. They have no defining characteristics; they are unproduced; they do not cease; they are unstained; they are not separate from stains. They do not decrease nor do they increase.

According to Tendar Lharampa these words indicate practice on the path of seeing. "All phenomena are empty," meaning they do not have any existence in and of themselves, constitutes the first door to liberation, the door of emptiness.

There are causal characteristics responsible for a thing's production and there are other characteristics which define a thing and allow us to posit it. These various characteristics exist, but not from their own side. Thus it says that things "have no defining characteristics." Results are produced and cease, but production and cessation lack signs of true existence. It therefore says "they are unproduced; they do not cease."

The afflicted side is that which is associated with the disturbing emotions and other mental stains. These stains exist but not inherently. It therefore says "they are unstained." The afflicted truths refer to true suffering and true sources of suffering. Something can be an afflicted phenomenon without being an afflicted truth. For instance, exalted Bodhisattvas on the first seven Bodhisattva stages[70] have not yet rid themselves of the misconception of true existence, which is an obstruction to liberation, but it can no longer act as a cause for further rebirth in cyclic existence and is therefore not a true source of suffering. The obstructions to omniscience also belong to the afflicted side.

The purified side of things is free from stains but not inherently so, which is why it says "they are not separate from stains." The purified truths refer to true cessations and true paths of insight. However, not everything that belongs to the purified side is a purified truth. Those on the paths of accumulation and preparation have actualized authentic paths of insight, which belong to the purified side, but these do not constitute the fourth noble truth, true paths, which refer to the paths of insight of the exalted. Emptiness belongs to the purified side, although it is not a purified truth, because through understanding it, purified truths are attained and it acts as a door to liberation.

These five aspects from "They have no defining characteristics" to "they are not separate from stains" constitute the second door to liberation, the door of signlessness, namely the absence of any truly existent signs or characteristics.

The faults of which we must rid ourselves decrease as we practice but there is no inherent decrease. Thus it says, "they do not decrease." The qualities we seek to develop increase in the course of our practice but they do not increase in terms of inherent existence. Thus it says "nor do they increase." These two aspects constitute the third door to liberation, the door of wishlessness. The doors of signlessness and of wishlessness can be subsumed within the door of emptiness and so, actually, there is only one door to liberation: the understanding of emptiness.

Gungtang Jampelyang's[71] classification of the first six aspects into the doors of emptiness and signlessness differs from Tendar Lharampa's presentation above. According to Gungtang, the fact that all phenomena are empty and that they have no inherently existent defining characteristics constitutes the door of emptiness. All phenomena associated with cyclic existence are products but they do not undergo any ultimate production or cessation. We aspire to attain a purified state but the mind is in fact unstained, since the stains have no ultimate existence. Natural nirvana, the emptiness of all things, is present in all phenomena from the very outset and so there is no inherently existent freedom or separation from stains. Following Gungtang, these four aspects constitute the door of signlessness. He does not specify anything different regarding the last two aspects which constitute the door of wishlessness.

No Conventional Phenomena

This being so, Shariputra, in emptiness there are no forms, no feelings, no discriminations, no compositional factors, no consciousnesses; no eyes, no ears, no nose, no tongue, no body, no mind; no visual forms, no sounds, no smells, no tastes, no tactile sensations, no mental objects. From the eye element to the mental element, right through to the element of mental consciousness—all do not exist. There is no ignorance and no ending of ignorance right through to no aging and death and also no ending of aging and death. In the same way there is no suffering, no source of suffering, no cessation, no path, no wisdom, no attainment, and no lack of attainment.

The profound paths of practice are the explicit subject-matter of the Perfection of Wisdom sutras and the extensive paths of practice are the hidden subject-matter. According to Gungtang Jampelyang, the part of the *Heart Sutra* which describes practice on the paths of accumulation and preparation is "Any sons or daughters of the noble lineage who want to perform the profound activity of perfecting wisdom should consider things in the following way." In this part the words "Any sons or daughters of the noble lineage who want to perform..." primarily indicate the path of accumulation of a person whose Mahayana disposition has awakened, who has developed the spirit of enlightenment and is engaged in creating the two great stores of merit and insight. The words "should consider things in the following way" then principally refer to practice on the path of preparation when reality is perceived by way of a mental image. Practice on the path of seeing extends from "They should clearly see that the five aggregates also are empty of inherent existence," near the beginning of Avalokiteshvara's answer, to "...no attainment and no lack of attainment."

The practitioner on the path of seeing directly experiences for the first time the emptiness of the five aggregates, the twelve sources, the eighteen constituents, and the twelve links of dependent arising, through which we remain in cyclic existence, in such a way that the emptiness appears clearly without the presence of any mental image. The perceiving awareness and that which is perceived are like water poured into water. They are of one taste, inasmuch as the meditator is no longer aware of any distinction between the awareness and its object. The path of meditation consists of familiarizing oneself with the emptiness of the phenomena mentioned above. Nothing new is added. This is why I favor Gungtang Jampelyang's interpretation, which includes on the path of seeing the classifications which cover all phenomena as the bases of emptiness. According to Tendar Lharampa, from "This being so, Shariputra..." to "...no attainment and no lack of attainment" describes practice on the path of meditation.

When direct perception of emptiness is gained, the disturbing emotions, though still present, no longer have the power to make us act in ways which will give rise to continued cyclic existence. Those on the Mahayana path of preparation and below create actions which keep them in cyclic existence. As has been mentioned, it is vital to develop the exalted understanding that the sphere of phenomena, emptiness, is present in all things, because it can rid us of true suffering and the true sources of suffering; but we should view this process as being simply attributed by terms and concepts and like an illusory lion killing an illusory elephant. The understanding which enables us to accomplish our aims and those aims themselves are merely like illusions. Beware though! This does not mean that they are non-existent.

When the orb of the sun has fully risen over the eastern horizon, it is complete but still has a long way to go before it reaches the zenith; and as it rises it gives off more and more heat. Similarly, everything that is to be seen regarding the nature of reality has been perceived on the path of seeing, but this insight will grow more powerful through the process of familiarization which takes place on the path of meditation. The distinction between the different Bodhisattva stages, which span the path of seeing and the path of meditation, is made on the basis of the skillful means accompanying meditative equipoise on emptiness. When a plane is in the air, its position cannot be determined in relation to the sky, which is like meditative equipoise on emptiness and always just sky. The plane's position is plotted in relation to the ground and the different countries over which it is passing.

Irrespective of the interpretation one follows regarding which parts of the sutra deal with the path of seeing and which with the path of meditation, on neither path do conventional phenomena appear to the awareness of the meditator in meditative equipoise directly perceiving reality.

Here, once again, there is mention of the five aggregates. Why, when they are mental factors, are feelings and discriminations singled out as special categories while all the other mental factors or activities are included within the aggregate of compositional factors?[72] In his *Treasury of Knowledge* Vasubandhu explains that discrimination in the form of adherence to ideologies or philosophical viewpoints is responsible for many conflicts. Might it not be better then to avoid adherence to any school of philosophical thought? Well, most of us don't need to worry about this, because we have not thought about the nature of reality in any depth and are not actually proponents of any philosophical tenets. True proponents of a philosophical view base their position on logical reasoning and are open to persuasion through the power of logic. Conflicts that do not arise from differences in ideology arise through attachment to happiness and pleasurable feelings and aversion to unhappiness and suffering. Thus feelings, too, act as a source of conflict and our attachment acts as a cause for further cyclic existence.

The words "no eyes, no ears, no nose, no tongue, no body, no mind; no visual forms, no sounds, no smells, no tastes, no tactile sensations, no mental objects" refer to the fact that in meditative equipoise during direct perception of reality the twelve sources, consisting of the five sense faculties and the mental faculty as well as the five kinds of sense objects and the objects of the mental faculty, do not appear to the meditator. Only their emptiness of inherent existence appears at that time.

"From the eye element to the mental element, right through to the element of mental consciousness—all do not exist" refers to the fact that the eighteen constituents do not appear either. These constituents consist of the six faculties, their six types of objects, and the six forms of consciousness which arise in dependence on these.

Neither do the twelve links or parts that constitute the process by which we remain in cyclic existence[73] appear during meditative equipoise. Ignorance, the first of these, is sometimes compared to darkness which hides forms. Similarly, it is said ignorance hides reality from us. For the Prasangikas ignorance not only hides but also distorts reality and is the misconception of the self and other things as truly existent. Everything appears truly existent to us and we assent to that appearance. From this the strong emotions of clinging attachment and hostility arise. This misconception is the fundamental form of ignorance. In addition there is also ignorance which is a wrong view regarding the connection between actions and their effects.

When we perform actions underlain by the misconception that the self is inherently existent as well as by a misunderstanding of the connection between actions and their effects, the action will be negative and will give rise to a bad rebirth. This applies particularly when our actions are motivated by the wish for happiness in this life. For instance, people perform blood sacrifices in the hope that it will bring them good fortune, which demonstrates their failure to understand correctly the connection between actions and their effects. If we have the basic misconception of how the self exists but are well motivated and perform a positive action, it will lead to a good rebirth but one within cyclic existence. These kinds of action are called formative action, the second link.

In the next moment the action ceases but it leaves an imprint on consciousness. The moment when that imprint is implanted is the third link, referred to as consciousness. Eventually when that imprint is triggered by craving and grasping, as will be described, conception occurs in the case of a rebirth from the womb. The moment of conception is called name and form, the fourth link. Form refers to the physical elements present, consisting of the father's sperm and the mother's ovum. Name refers to the other four aggregates which are present in potential form.

As the fetus becomes firm the six sources—the five sense faculties and the mental faculty—develop. This is the fifth link. Through the development of the six sources, contact, the sixth link, occurs. Contact between a sense faculty, an object, and consciousness produces the ability to experience objects and leads to the seventh link, feeling and sensation, which may be pleasurable, painful, or neutral.

The eighth link, craving, which is an aspect of attachment, triggers the imprint that was implanted on consciousness by the formative action. This craving may be the wish not to be separated from pleasurable feelings or to be separated from painful ones. The ninth link, grasping, is a heightened form of craving and is directed towards the sense objects or towards misguided forms of discipline and conduct. It can be an adherence to the false view of the transitory collection as a real I and mine or can be directed towards other wrong views. When the imprint is fully activated through craving and grasping, everything is ready for the next rebirth. This state of readiness is the tenth link, existence. Then the development in the womb from the fourth to the seventh links takes place, as has been described above. When this is concluded, birth from the womb, the eleventh link, occurs, followed by aging and death, the twelfth link. In fact, however, aging begins the moment after conception.

This twelve-part process associated with the afflicted side, namely how we remain in cyclic existence, is usually contemplated in forward sequence and reverse sequence. In forward sequence we consider how a moment of ignorance leads through all of these steps to birth and then aging and death. In reverse sequence we retrace the steps from aging and death back to ignorance. Meditation on the process associated with the purified side in forward sequence entails looking at how by stopping ignorance we stop formative action and through this stop everything that follows. In reverse sequence we look at how aging and death are stopped by stopping birth and so forth back to the stopping of ignorance.

During meditative equipoise on the nature of reality none of these conventional phenomena appear to the meditator. This is why the sutra says "There is no ignorance and no ending of ignorance right through to no aging and death and no ending of aging and death." Only the emptiness of all this appears. The fact that none of these phenomena appear does not, however, mean that they have been perceived to be non-existent.

Next the sutra mentions the four noble truths, which also do not appear during meditative equipoise on reality. Even the wisdom itself, the direct perception of emptiness, does not appear to the meditator because it, too, is a conventional phenomenon. For the practitioner at this point, the mind cognizing emptiness and its object are indistinguishable. The ten powers and the four kinds of fearlessness[74] are among the attainments of an enlightened being, but neither these nor the lack of them appears. This concludes the general description of practice on the path of meditation according to Tendar Lharampa's presentation.

He points out that one of the reasons for itemizing these diverse bases of emptiness in the form of the five aggregates, the twelve sources, and the eighteen constituents is to counter the assertions of various Indian non-Buddhist schools regarding the nature of the self. For instance, some assert that the inner self or person is a conscious entity distinct from the body but residing within it. This conscious entity looks out through the doors of the senses rather like a monkey in a room with several windows. Though it appears from the outside as if there are a number of monkeys, there is, according to this view, actually only one running back and forth, first appearing at one window and then at another.

The classification of all the different kinds of consciousness and the factors necessary to produce them counters such an idea. It also counters the assertion that this conscious inner being is permanent because it is unproduced and does not disintegrate, unitary because it lacks parts of any kind, and independent because it does not rely on any causes and conditions. From a Buddhist perspective, ideas of a self that remains bound in cyclic existence or gains freedom as an entity distinct from the aggregates are intellectually formed misconceptions.

Those who assert the existence of a self-sufficient substantially existent self say that the thought I arises quite spontaneously without depending on any other factors—just as the perception of blue requires only the presence of blue and nothing further—and thus the self is substantially existent. Most Buddhist schools of thought, other than the Prasangika, consider such an idea of a self-sufficient substantially existent self as the innate misconception of the self.

Buddhist proponents of philosophical tenets assert that the person is imputedly existent because it is impossible to conceive of the person without depending on the aggregates. They argue that there is no self-sufficient substantially existent person independent of parts or a collection of parts because such a person cannot be found as either identical with or separate from the aggregates and is therefore as non-existent as a rabbit's horn. However, apart from the Prasangikas, they assert that the aggregates are substantially existent and when one seeks for what will serve as an exemplification of the self, it can be found among the aggregates. Prasangikas assert that everything which exists does so imputedly and that nothing has any substantial existence or can be found when a search for it is made.

From a Prasangika standpoint the misconception that the person is a self-sufficient substantially existent entity can be intellectually formed or innate, but in both cases it is a coarse misconception. In its coarsest form the self and the aggregates are seen as having different characteristics and being like a king and his court or like a shepherd who is in charge of his sheep but not one of them. The Prasangikas consider this as tantamount to asserting the existence of a permanent, unitary, independent self.

Where the innate misconception of a self-sufficient substantially existent person is concerned, according to the Prasangikas, the self and the aggregates are seen as sharing the same characteristics, yet the self is in control of the aggregates in the same way that the head trader shares the attributes of the other traders but is nevertheless in charge of them. Prasangikas do not consider either of these misconceptions as the fundamental misconception of the self, which is a conception that the self is truly existent. The understanding that there is no self-sufficient substantially existent self is for them an understanding of coarse selflessness and is not an understanding of emptiness.[75]

Therefore, Shariputra, since Bodhisattvas have no attainment, they depend upon and dwell in the perfection of wisdom.

These words describe the vajra-like meditative stabilization of Bodhisattvas on the tenth stage, who have attained the exalted wisdom which marks the end of their existence as sentient beings. For them all elaborations have been pacified and they are in a state of meditative equipoise which is similar to that of an enlightened being who will never again arise from that state. It is, however, not yet the fully fledged meditative equipoise of an enlightened being because although that practitioner has actualized the direct antidote to the most subtle obstructions to knowledge of all phenomena, these obstructions have not yet been eliminated in such a way that they can never again return. It is as if the thief has been thrown out of the house but the door must now be shut behind him.

Since their minds are without obstructions, they have no fear. Going beyond all distortions, they finally reach the state beyond sorrow, the culmination. All Buddhas of the past, present, and future have depended, do, and will depend upon the perfection of wisdom, through which they become unsurpassable perfectly and completely awakened Buddhas.

This describes the path of no more learning. Through the process which takes place on the path of meditation the obstructions to knowledge of all phenomena are progressively eliminated. Because all obstructions have now been removed, all fear has come to an end. The distortions of holding what is impermanent to be permanent, what is painful to be pleasurable, what is unclean to be clean, and what is selfless to exist in and of itself, as well as all imprints and traces of these misconceptions, have been totally eliminated, and the state beyond the extremes of worldly existence and personal peace has been attained. This is the way all Buddhas of the past and of the present have practiced and how all future Buddhas will practice in order to attain the highest state of enlightenment.

Tendar Lharampa states that the whole section from "Therefore, Shariputra, since Bodhisattvas have no attainment..." to "...they become unsurpassable perfectly and completely awakened Buddhas" describes the path of no more learning. Gungtang Rinpoche says that the passage "...since Bodhisattvas have no attainment, they depend upon and dwell in the perfection of wisdom. Their minds are without obstructions and fears. Going beyond all distortions, they finally reach the state beyond sorrow, the culmination" describes the path of meditation and that the words "All Buddhas of the past, present, and future have depended, do, and will depend upon the perfection of wisdom, through which they become unsurpassable perfectly and completely awakened Buddhas" describe the vajra-like meditative stabilization at the end of the path of meditation as well as the path of no more learning.

THE MANTRA

Therefore, the mantra of the perfection of wisdom is a mantra of great knowledge. It is an unsurpassable mantra, a mantra comparable to the incomparable. It is a mantra that totally pacifies all suffering. It will not deceive you, therefore know that it is true! I proclaim the mantra of the perfection of wisdom: *DAYATA (OM) GATE GATE PARAGATE PARASAMGATE BODHI SWAHA.*

Because the *Heart Sutra* contains a mantra there has been extensive discussion by the commentators about whether it should be classified as a sutra teaching or as a teaching of secret mantra. In both sutra and tantra the final object is the same—to attain the body, speech, and mind of an enlightened being. Although the complete path to enlightenment is laid out from a sutra point of view in the *Heart Sutra*, the introduction of the mantra indicates that when the essential realizations have been gained, it is necessary to engage in tantric practice in order to attain enlightenment. Tendar Lharampa states that it is difficult to decide how the *Heart Sutra* should be classified, while Gungtang Jampelyang says it should be considered as a sutra teaching because the practice of secret mantra is merely indicated.

A mantra is that which protects the mind. Through this mantra, which is the perfection of wisdom itself, we can overcome the demon of ignorance that possesses us and find unsurpassable happiness. It protects the minds of those who practice it from all fears and describes how to make the transition from worldly existence to the supreme state beyond sorrow. It is a mantra of great knowledge because it saves us from the poison of ignorance and its imprints. It is an unsurpassable mantra because it frees us from suffering and its causes as no other path of insight can. The incomparable is the state beyond suffering. Since it helps us to attain that state, it is comparable to the incomparable. It totally pacifies suffering because it rids us of all the troubles of the world and their causes. The world here refers to ordinary beings like us. Our troubles are many but foremost are birth, aging, sickness, and death. This mantra does not deceive us and it is true because wisdom sees things as they actually are without any error or deception. It is therefore transcendent.

This description of the mantra also sets out the five paths. Thus "the mantra of the perfection of wisdom" refers to the path of accumulation; "a mantra of great knowledge" to the path of preparation; "an unsurpassable mantra" to the path of seeing; "a mantra comparable to the incomparable" to the path of meditation; and "a mantra that totally pacifies all suffering" to the path of no more learning. When we have actualized these five paths, we are totally protected.

The mantra itself means, "It is thus: go, go, go beyond, go completely beyond, establish the foundation of enlightenment." Sometimes *DAYATA* is included only in the first recitation and omitted in subsequent recitations. Gungtang Jampelyang comments extensively on *DAYATA*, meaning "it is thus." The Buddha trained himself in everything associated with goodness and virtue over a long period of time. He learned to cherish others more than himself and through this his Mahayana disposition awakened. His great compassion extended towards all living beings without making distinctions between them and his heart was filled with the wish to free them.

He saw clearly that our misconceptions of the self are what bind us to cyclic existence, but he realized that without freeing himself from those misconceptions, he would not be able to liberate others. Therefore, he gained prolonged familiarity with the understanding of selflessness until he was able to rid himself not only of the obstructions formed by misconceptions regarding the self and other phenomena, which prevent complete insight into the fundamental way in which things exist, but also of their imprints. He then was able to perceive all phenomena in the most clear and perfect way.

He understood that there is no other road those who wish to train themselves can take, other than the one he had taken. *It is thus:* The true middle way is the union of emptiness and dependent arising, which precludes the two extremes of reified existence and non-existence. He taught this from his own experience without relying on another, which demonstrates his authenticity and shows him to be an unsurpassable teacher. The greatness of the teacher indicates the validity of the teaching—in this case the Perfection of Wisdom sutras. When we imagine the objects of refuge before us, we do not visualize something unattainable. The Buddha was once like us and we can become like him, for we, too, have the potential to attain enlightenment.

Happiness and suffering depend upon the mind. This is why the great Indian master Nagarjuna in his *Letter to a Friend* tells his friend the king:

Tame your mind. The Subduer has perfectly explained
That the root of the teachings is the mind.

The crux of the matter is that we must learn to control our minds. This is the keystone of the Buddha's teachings. Our minds create both cyclic existence and the state beyond sorrow, so in that respect the two states are the same. But there is a distinction between them: one is superior, the other inferior. The state we are in depends upon whether our perception is mistaken or not. Mistaken means that what we perceive does not accord with fact and unmistaken means that it does accord with fact. We must come to know things as they actually are and thereby rid ourselves of wrong perceptions. We must find the middle path well away from the abyss of the two extremes, for this is the only door to peace.

The fundamental middle is emptiness itself. First we must establish that this is how things exist. The middle path is the understanding of emptiness and through cultivating it we can reach the resultant middle,[76] the state of complete enlightenment free from the extreme states of worldly existence and personal peace. The focal object, emptiness, is present in the multiplicity of existent phenomena. When we gain the exalted understanding of emptiness, we have gained an inconceivably vast insight and accomplishment because we have directly understood the fundamental nature of everything that exists. Wherever there is space, there are living beings who suffer. When we develop compassion which embraces all of these living beings without discriminating between them, that, too, is an inconceivably vast accomplishment.

Emptiness, which is present in everything that exists, always has the same identity. *It is thus:* During meditative equipoise on the fundamental nature of things, that nature is experienced directly in a non-dual way, as having the same taste, without distinctions or elaborations, no matter what the basis of emptiness may be. It is experienced just as it is. This is the essence of the Perfection of Wisdom sutras and reveals the greatness of the quintessential and explicit subject-matter of the Perfection of Wisdom sutras, consisting of the profound.

The Buddha perfected every good quality and experienced

a sublime state of existence. We ordinary people experience the miseries of cyclic existence. This difference does not come about through external factors, nor has any other power or being created it. It is entirely due to previous actions, which determine what we experience.

Ordinary living beings long for happiness but constantly pursue the causes of suffering. The Buddha did the opposite. He clearly understood what gives rise to happiness and what produces suffering and acted accordingly. His transformation did not take place in an instant but through a gradual step-by-step process which eventually led to his enlightenment. *It is thus:* All past Buddhas have gone to enlightenment in this way and we must do likewise. This, also, shows the greatness of the teaching and indicates the hidden aspect of the Perfection of Wisdom sutras, consisting of the stages of the path associated with the extensive side of practice.

Gungtang Rinpoche advises us to think carefully and deeply about our present condition and why we are in this state, about where we would like to be and how we can get there. Where are we at present? Firmly entrenched in cyclic existence with a contaminated body and mind that are the result of compulsive actions underlain by the disturbing emotions. Our possessions, our friends, and the places where we live are all somehow or other associated with suffering and unhappiness. As long as we remain in cyclic existence, we will never find true and lasting happiness. It is like a needle. No matter from which side you touch the point, it always pricks. And it is like a heap of excrement, which continues to smell foul as long as it is there—to hope that it will ever smell nice is futile.

This contaminated body and mind are the main exemplification of true suffering and they are the result of ignorance and the formative actions which stem from it. Our craving for ordinary pleasures keeps us fettered because it prevents us from clearly seeing the dimensions of our present suffering. As long as we do not recognize suffering as suffering and remain enthralled by these pleasures, we will behave carelessly and will never begin the task of freeing ourselves.

Where are we going? To liberation, which is the state beyond sorrow, where all the suffering of cyclic existence has stopped. The mere cessation of contaminated actions and the disturbing emotions, which halts the cycle of involuntary birth and death, is the enlightenment of the lesser vehicle. The ending of even the imprints of ignorance is the supreme form of cessation, free from the two extremes and adorned with the fulfillment of our own highest aims and with the ability to fulfill the needs of others. This is the ultimate accomplishment.

How do we get there? That which eventually reaches the state beyond sorrow is the reality of our minds with stains. The principal true path of insight is the exalted non-conceptual direct understanding which perceives with clarity that all phenomena are free from inherent existence. Similar to this is the conceptual understanding which comprehends the fundamental nature of things clearly via a mental image. This is, as it were, the retainer of the principal path of insight. Paths of insight regarding imperma- nence and suffering lead to the essential understanding of reali- ty. In the same way, it is said that the practice of the first five perfections is for the sake of the sixth, the perfection of wisdom.

It is very helpful to know all the stages of the path and to take them to mind frequently on our meditation cushion be- cause with sufficient familiarity we will come to see how they are all interconnected. If we want to describe an elephant to someone who has never seen one, speaking only about its trunk and tusks will give the wrong impression and the person might think an elephant is something long and tubular like an intes- tine with sharp points. But if we describe the elephant fully, when the person actually comes across an elephant, he will instantly recognize it. We should know and keep reminding ourselves of the entire path but we must practice what we have a pro- pensity for and what is appropriate to our particular stage of development.

Although *OM* is often omitted in the printed versions of the mantra, many great masters in their commentaries say it should be included. The syllable *OM* is a sacred syllable for Buddhists and Hindus alike and imbues the mantra with power. For Buddhists, arousing the right kind of intention, reciting the syllable *OM*, and remembering what it represents, is in itself a powerful prac- tice. Some say that even just reciting the syllable with no deeper knowledge of its significance is of value because of its sacredness.

OM consists of three sounds: *a, o* and *m.* These three represent the vajra body, speech, and mind of enlightened beings. The three are definitive and are what we seek to accomplish. They also symbolize all the practices that act as causes for the attainment of the body, speech, and mind of an enlightened being, which can be classified as those which increase skillful means and those which increase insight and wisdom. From the sutra point of view the former produce the vajra body and vajra speech, while the latter produce vajra mind.

There are four classes of tantra. Action tantra and performance tantra are the two lower classes, while yoga tantra and highest yoga tantra are the two upper classes. In the action and performance tantras the paths of practice are said to be with signs and without signs. According to Gungtang Rinpoche those with signs give rise to vajra body and speech and those without signs to vajra mind.[77]

In yoga tantra there are four seals.[78] The aim is to purify our ordinary body, speech, mind, and activities; the ordinary elements of earth, fire, water, and air; and desire, confusion, hostility, and avarice. The body is purified by the great seal, speech by the teaching seal, the mind by the commitment seal, and ordinary activities by the action seal. In each case the practice involves what is symbolized and the symbols that represent it.

In the context of the great seal the body of the deity is what is symbolized. The hand gesture made by the deity is the external symbol, and imagining ourselves in the physical form of the deity is the internal symbol.

The sixty qualities of the deity's speech are what is symbolized with regard to the teaching seal. Imagining ourselves as the deity with our tongue and throat marked by sacred seed syllables is the external symbol. Imagining the form of those syllables as their sound is the internal symbol.

The non-conceptual exalted wisdom of the deity's mind in the form of a ritual implement is what is symbolized in the commitment seal. Making gestures with this implement is the external symbol and imagining ourselves as the deity in possession of this wisdom is the internal symbol.

As for the action seal, the deity's enlightened activities and blessings are what is represented. Imagining ourselves as the deity emanating and reabsorbing rays of light is the external symbol, and the internal one consists of imagining ourselves effortlessly and spontaneously performing the enlightened activities of the deity. Through the practice of the four seals on the path we accomplish the resultant four seals: the wisdom truth body, the enjoyment body, the emanation body, and the nature body of an enlightened being.

Highest yoga tantra consists of two stages: the generation stage and the completion stage.[79] The practices of the former yield the vajra body. The practices of the completion stage associated with the conventional illusory body produce vajra speech and those associated with the ultimate clear light produce vajra mind. Since *OM* then symbolizes vajra body, speech, and mind and all the practices which give rise to them, even one recitation of this sacred syllable is of great value.

The first *GATE* refers to the path of accumulation, the second to the path of preparation, *PARAGATE* to the path of seeing, *PARASAMGATE* to the path of meditation, and *BODHI SVAHA* to the path of no more learning. The five paths here are posited not in terms of skillful means but of wisdom. On the path of accumulation, we accumulate the causes which will eventually give rise to the clear appearance of emptiness, the fundamental nature of everything existent. On the path of preparation, we see the nature of reality clearly though still in terms of a mental image. On the path of seeing, emptiness is seen with complete clarity for the first time. On the path of meditation, the practitioner repeatedly gains familiarity with this clear perception, and when everything has been perfected the path of no more learning is reached.

To make their practice powerful Bodhisattvas on the paths of accumulation and preparation must combine their cultivation of the perfection of wisdom with skillful means. Those who have reached the Bodhisattva stages undertake thorough training[80] in overcoming and purifying themselves of all faults and limitations and developing the prerequisite realizations by constantly combining skillful means and wisdom.

GATE GATE PARAGATE PARASAMGATE has been translated as "go, go, go beyond, go completely beyond." Gungtang

Rinpoche states that this should not be regarded as an imperative to go from one path to another but to go towards enlightenment by means of each of the paths, like travelling across the sea in a ship. The imperative is used to indicate that greater and greater qualities must all definitely be accomplished. Finally there is no more going but only the arrival or manifestation of complete enlightenment.

The syllables *P* and *Bf PH* introduce the concept of here and beyond. The demarcation between here and beyond is the juncture when we become exalted beings. When the sun of directly understanding reality dawns, we become free of the three fetters which bind us. These three are the false view of the transitory collection as a real I and mine, holding wrong forms of discipline and conduct as supreme, and deluded doubt.[81] The sun of directly understanding reality dispels the cold dark shadows of suffering created by our involvement with these three. This is the state beyond our present one, in which because of this darkness and cold we are driven from one rebirth to another by contaminated actions underlain by disturbing emotions.

The rising sun on the eastern horizon and the sun at the zenith are both the same sun, but the higher it rises in the sky, the stronger its heat and light. *PH* and *PHE* describe an incremental progression as greater and greater familiarity with the direct understanding of emptiness is gained. The first two repetitions of *PHE* refer to the two paths which are on this side as opposed to the other side, which is that of exalted beings.

As we have seen, the essence of the Buddha's teachings is contained in the Perfection of Wisdom sutras, the shortest of which is the *Heart Sutra*, and the pith of the *Heart Sutra* is contained in the mantra. So we can say the mantra sums up the eighty-four thousand different teachings of the Buddha, and if we practice this mantra we are practicing the quintessence of all these different teachings and will experience the benefits of doing so.

At the beginning of the *Heart Sutra* the scene is set at Vulture's Peak outside the town of Rajgir with the Buddha and the great Bodhisattva Avalokiteshvara both absorbed in meditation. Avalokiteshvara is meditating on the nature of reality when, inspired by the Buddha, Shariputra questions him about how to cultivate the perfection of wisdom. Not only does this indicate the importance of receiving teachings that have been passed down as part of a living tradition, it also shows that we need intelligence and a questioning mind if we are to get to the true meaning of the instructions. In Buddhism it is considered vital that what we practice should have its source in the Buddha's teaching and that the instructions should have come down to us in an unbroken continuity of oral transmission, passed from one living person to another. The warmth of the blessings is thus sustained and never dies.

But it is not enough merely to receive the teachings in this way. We also need the intelligence and energy to understand them and put them into practice. We all have very different capacities, dispositions, and unfulfilled potential. The problem is that we see everything through a haze of distortions and idle away our life as if everything were fine.

The disturbing attitudes and emotions are the cause of all our suffering and it is through understanding reality that we can rid ourselves of them, yet only very few of us have anything more than a superficial interest in understanding reality. That sense of urgency and the willingness to invest every ounce of our energy in our quest is missing. Have we ever met anyone totally dedicated to discovering how things actually exist? It is rare to find people who are even fully conversant with the terminology used to refer to these matters.

So often we feel bored and uninterested when spiritual practice is mentioned. We have an aversion to the word "virtue" and prefer other more palatable words that convey the same idea. Though the means for alleviating our suffering are at hand, we shy away from them. If we had enough conviction to practice with energy and enthusiasm, we would begin to experience some results and that would give us a great incentive to continue.

Having completed his explanation, Avalokiteshvara says:

Shariputra, it is in this way that Bodhisattvas, those great beings, train themselves in the profound perfection of wisdom.

THE CONCLUSION AND COLOPHON

Then the Victor arose from his concentration and expressed his approval to the Bodhisattva, that great being, the exalted and powerful Avalokiteshvara, "Well said, well said! Son of the noble lineage, that is just how it is, just how it is. The profound perfection of wisdom should be practiced exactly as you have explained it. Then the Tathagatas will rejoice."

Although enlightened beings never actually arise from meditative equipoise, to ordinary appearances the Buddha now arises from the concentration in which he has been absorbed and expresses his appreciation and approval. He says that the perfection of wisdom is exactly as Avalokiteshvara has explained it and just as he, the Buddha, has understood it to be. This is how we must train ourselves and if we do so, it will delight the enlightened ones of the ten directions and they will all rejoice. First we must gain some understanding of the subject-matter of the Perfection of Wisdom sutras and then try to practice what we have understood.

When the Victor had spoken these words, the venerable Shariputra and the Bodhisattva, that great being, the exalted and powerful Avalokiteshvara, and the entire gathering as well as the worlds of gods, humans, demi-gods, and celestial musicians rejoiced, and they praised what the Victor had said.

Colophon

This concludes the Mahayana sutra known as *The Essence of the Perfection of Wisdom, the Victorious.* It was translated by the Indian abbot Vimalamitra[82] and by the fully ordained translator Rinchen Dey. It was revised and finalized by the fully ordained great reviser and translator Namka and others. The excellently revised [version] was written on the wall of Geygyey Chema Ling in the temple [complex] Lhungyi Drupa of glorious Samyey.[83]

The sutra consists of three parts: the introduction or prologue, which has a general and a specific section; the body of the sutra; and the above conclusion. This is followed by the colophon, which supplies details regarding the translation of the sutra into Tibetan. The introduction and conclusion are referred to as "permitted words" which have been included by the compiler of the sutra. The exchange between Shariputra and Avalokiteshvara is termed "blessed words," and of course the part where the Enlightened One expresses his approval consists of words from the Buddha's own mouth.

The *Heart Sutra* is considered to be of great importance in the Mahayana tradition. Think about its content with a really open mind and if you find something in it that you consider of value, cherish that; otherwise, leave it aside. If you feel drawn to it, the essential thing is to make it part of your own mind. That has happened when what you perceive and think eventually comes into line with what the text says. At present there is a gap between our minds and the teachings large enough for a train to pass through. That means our faith and aspiration are superficial, like lung which floats on top of the water when it's cooking. If we approach the teachings in a shallow way, they cannot grip us and we will soon feel bored.

The root of all our ills, as we have seen, is the misconception of the self. Although the entirety of the Buddha's teachings is medicine to cure these ills, his explanation of emptiness and dependent arising is the supreme panacea. Once emptiness has been understood directly, the disturbing emotions no longer have the power to influence our actions and we will never again act in ways that are driven by ignorance regarding the nature of the self. This will end the whole process by which we remain trapped in our present condition.

According to Buddhist cosmology, when a world system comes into existence, first there is space and then form comes into being. Through a movement of energy, water vapor and condensation occur. The water is then churned and matter solidifies. The formation and existence of physical matter and living beings is only possible because of this space. When a world system disintegrates, various phenomena such as violent floods, winds, and conflagrations occur. And then once more there is space. The nature of the space before the world system came into existence is no different from the space that is there when the world system has disintegrated. It is, as it were, the basis for both the evolution and devolution of the world system.

Our minds are space-like in that they are empty of intrinsic existence and have a clear and cognizant nature. Because the mind has this open quality, the movement of thoughts is possible. This is like the movement of energy in the formation of a world system. Among these thoughts are those which are characterized by an incorrect approach from which the disturbing emotions arise. They and our contaminated actions are like the water which is churned. The solid matter that forms is our body and our world, the outcome of the churning. Aging, sickness, and death follow birth just as the disintegration of a world system is marked by various violent phenomena. Whether we are coming into existence or going out of existence, the clear light nature of the mind remains unchanged and unaffected. It is this clear light nature of the mind that allows us to rid ourselves of distorting misconceptions and to develop marvelous qualities.

Our thoughts are like bubbles that rise from the water and vanish back into it or like clouds that form and disappear in the sky. They, like our thoughts, do not come from anywhere nor go anywhere. When we rid ourselves of the disturbing emotions and attitudes, they disappear right there within the nature of our minds. The point where they end within the reality of the mind is true cessation, the third noble truth. We should never forget about the clear light nature of our minds.

The fact that things are free from intrinsic existence and depend on causes and conditions has extremely encouraging implications. We all have limitations and faults which we need to overcome, and there are many abilities and qualities we wish to develop and strengthen. None of these is intrinsically existent and all depend on causes and conditions, which means that we can do something even now to free ourselves from the faults and to develop these qualities. Once we have discovered this for ourselves and know it to be true, instead of thinking that it is just something which is said in the Buddhist teachings, we will feel a genuine wish to make some effort and our involvement with the teachings will be more than mere play-acting.

In the different spiritual traditions of the world there is mention of great practitioners and of the places where they lived and practiced, but who is there of comparable excellence today? The very same teachings which they put into practice are available to us now and the power of those teachings has not diminished. But when people stop practicing them, the teachings eventually die out, and once a spiritual tradition is dying, it is very difficult to revive. The teachings don't remain out there somewhere, waving in the wind like a flag. They only thrive in the mind-streams of human beings.

While there are people who are studying the teachings of a particular religious tradition, thinking about them, integrating them through meditation and transforming themselves by making their minds more peaceful and benevolent, that religion is flourishing. This, not the number of adherents it has, is the true indicator. For though the number of adherents can determine its material wealth, they may simply follow that religion out of bias but know very little about it and have even less interest in actually practicing it. The health of a religion can be measured by the number of individuals committed to its practice and by the joy it kindles in the heart because of the benefit it brings to the world. To benefit living beings and the world in which they live is the true purpose of all authentic spiritual traditions.

There are still people who through their practice have gained personal conviction and knowledge of the teachings embodied in the *Heart Sutra*, but they too will be dead one day. This knowledge will disappear with them unless young people take sufficient interest in time. There are many kinds of knowledge but the most important is the understanding of emptiness, the mother whom we should lovingly embrace. Knowledge and practice must go hand in hand. Just knowledge without practice will not yield the desired results, but how can we practice unless we understand what needs to be done? Combining both is the way to perfect wisdom.

THE ROOT TEXT:

THE HEART SUTRA

The following words are not part of the Heart Sutra *but are often recited beforehand.*

Homage to the mother of the Victors of the three times—
To the perfection of wisdom beyond thought
    and expression,
Unborn, unceasing, in the nature of space,
The object of the exalted wisdom which knows itself.

THE HEART SUTRA

In the Indian language: *Bhagavatīprajñāpāramitāhṛdaya*
In the Tibetan language: *bCom ldan 'das ma shes rab kyi pha
    rol tu phyin pa'i snying po*
[In the English language: *The Essence of the Perfection of
    Wisdom, the Victorious*]

The Heart Sutra

One section

Homage to the Perfection of Wisdom, the Victorious.

Thus I have heard. At one time the Victor was at Vulture's Peak near Rajgir together with a great assembly of the fully ordained and a great assembly of Bodhisattvas. On that occasion the Victor was absorbed in a concentration on the diversity of phenomena called "profound appearance." Also at that time the Bodhisattva, that great being, the exalted and powerful Avalokiteshvara was contemplating the profound practice of the perfection of wisdom, and he saw that the five aggregates, too, are empty of any inherent nature.

Then, through the power of the Buddha, the venerable Shariputra asked the Bodhisattva, that great being, the exalted and powerful Avalokiteshvara, "How should any child of the noble lineage who wants to perform the profound activity of perfecting wisdom proceed?"

The Bodhisattva, that great being, the exalted and powerful Avalokiteshvara answered the venerable Shariputra, saying, "Any sons or daughters of the noble lineage who want to perform the profound activity of perfecting wisdom should consider things in the following way. They should clearly see that the five aggregates also are empty of any inherent nature. Form is empty.

Emptiness is form. Emptiness is not other than form and form is not other than emptiness. Similarly, feelings, discriminations, compositional factors, and consciousnesses are also empty. Likewise, Shariputra, all phenomena are empty. They have no defining characteristics; they are unproduced; they do not cease; they are unstained; they are not separate from stains. They do not decrease nor do they increase.

"This being so, Shariputra, in emptiness there are no forms, no feelings, no discriminations, no compositional factors, no consciousnesses; no eyes, no ears, no nose, no tongue, no body, no mind; no visual forms, no sounds, no smells, no tastes, no tactile sensations, no mental objects. From the eye element to the mental element, right through to the element of mental consciousness—all do not exist. There is no ignorance and no ending of ignorance right through to no aging and death and also no ending of aging and death. In the same way there is no suffering, no source of suffering, no cessation, no path, no wisdom, no attainment, and no lack of attainment.

"Therefore, Shariputra, since Bodhisattvas have no attainment, they depend upon and dwell in the perfection of wisdom. Since their minds are without obstructions, they have no fear. Going beyond all distortions, they finally reach the state beyond sorrow, the culmination.

"All Buddhas of the past, present, and future have depended, do, and will depend upon the perfection of wisdom, through which they become unsurpassable perfectly and completely awakened Buddhas.

"Therefore, the mantra of the perfection of wisdom is a mantra of great knowledge. It is an unsurpassable mantra, a mantra comparable to the incomparable. It is a mantra that totally pacifies all suffering. It will not deceive you, therefore know that it is true! I proclaim the mantra of the perfection of wisdom: *DAYATA (OM) GATE GATE PARAGATE PARASAMGATE BODHI SWAHA.* Shariputra, it is in this way that Bodhisattvas, those great beings, train themselves in the profound perfection of wisdom."

Then the Victor arose from his concentration and expressed his approval to the Bodhisattva, that great being, the exalted and powerful Avalokiteshvara, "Well said, well said! Son of the noble lineage, that is just how it is, just how it is. The profound perfection of wisdom should be practiced exactly as you have explained it. Then the Tathagatas will rejoice."

When the Victor had spoken these words, the venerable Shariputra and the Bodhisattva, that great being, the exalted and powerful Avalokiteshvara, and the entire gathering as well as the worlds of gods, humans, demi-gods, and celestial musicians rejoiced, and they praised what the Victor had said.

The Root Text: The Heart Sutra

Colophon
This concludes the Mahayana sutra known as *The Essence of the Perfection of Wisdom, the Victorious.* It was translated by the Indian abbot Vimalamitra and by the fully ordained translator Rinchen Dey. It was revised and finalized by the fully ordained great reviser and translator Namka and others. The excellently revised [version] was written on the wall of Geygyey Chema Ling in the temple [complex] Lhungyi Drupa of glorious Samyey.

THE TIBETAN TEXT

༄༅།། བཅོམ་ལྡན་འདས་མ་ཤེས་རབ་ཀྱི་ཕ་རོལ་ཏུ་ཕྱིན་པའི་སྙིང་པོ་ཞེས་བྱ་བ་བཞུགས་སོ།།

༄༅།། རྒྱ་གར་སྐད་དུ། བྷ་ག་བ་ཏི་པྲ་ཛྙཱ་པཱ་ར་མི་ཏཱ་ཧྲྀ་ད་ཡ།།
བོད་སྐད་དུ། བཅོམ་ལྡན་འདས་མ་ཤེས་རབ་ཀྱི་ཕ་རོལ་ཏུ་ཕྱིན་པའི་སྙིང་པོ།།

བམ་པོ་གཅིག་གོ།

བཅོམ་ལྡན་འདས་མ་ཤེས་རབ་ཀྱི་ཕ་རོལ་ཏུ་ཕྱིན་པ་ལ་ཕྱག་འཚལ་ལོ། འདི་སྐད་བདག་གིས་
ཐོས་པ་དུས་གཅིག་ན། བཅོམ་ལྡན་འདས་རྒྱལ་པོའི་ཁབ་ན་བྱ་རྒོད་ཀྱི་ཕུང་པོའི་རི་ལ་དགེ་སློང་གི་དགེ་
འདུན་ཆེན་པོ་དང་། བྱང་ཆུབ་སེམས་དཔའི་དགེ་འདུན་ཆེན་པོ་དང་ཐབས་གཅིག་ཏུ་བཞུགས་ཏེ།
དེའི་ཚེ་བཅོམ་ལྡན་འདས་ཟབ་མོ་སྣང་བ་ཞེས་བྱ་བའི་ཆོས་ཀྱི་རྣམ་གྲངས་ཀྱི་ཏིང་ངེ་འཛིན་ལ་སྙོམས་པར་
བཞུགས་སོ། ཡང་དེའི་ཚེ་བྱང་ཆུབ་སེམས་དཔའ་སེམས་དཔའ་ཆེན་པོ་འཕགས་པ་སྤྱན་རས་གཟིགས་
དབང་ཕྱུག་ཤེས་རབ་ཀྱི་ཕ་རོལ་ཏུ་ཕྱིན་པ་ཟབ་མོའི་སྤྱོད་པ་ཉིད་ལ་རྣམ་པར་བལྟ་ཞིང་། ཕུང་པོ་ལྔ་པོ་
དག་ལ་ཡང་རང་བཞིན་གྱིས་སྟོང་པར་རྣམ་པར་ལྟོ། དེ་ནས་སངས་རྒྱས་ཀྱི་མཐུས། ཚེ་དང་ལྡན་
པ་ཤཱ་རིའི་བུས། བྱང་ཆུབ་སེམས་དཔའ་སེམས་དཔའ་ཆེན་པོ་འཕགས་པ་སྤྱན་རས་གཟིགས་དབང་
ཕྱུག་ལ་འདི་སྐད་ཅེས་སྨྲས་སོ། རིགས་ཀྱི་བུ་གང་ལ་ལ་ཤེས་རབ་ཀྱི་ཕ་རོལ་ཏུ་ཕྱིན་པ་ཟབ་མོའི་སྤྱོད་པ་
སྤྱད་པར་འདོད་པ་དེས་ཇི་ལྟར་བསླབ་པར་བྱ། དེ་སྐད་ཅེས་སྨྲས་པ་དང་། བྱང་ཆུབ་སེམས་དཔའ་
སེམས་དཔའ་ཆེན་པོ་འཕགས་པ་སྤྱན་རས་གཟིགས་དབང་ཕྱུག་གིས་ཚེ་དང་ལྡན་པ་ཤཱ་རིའི་བུ་ལ་འདི་
སྐད་ཅེས་སྨྲས་སོ། ཤཱ་རིའི་བུ། རིགས་ཀྱི་བུའམ་རིགས་ཀྱི་བུ་མོ་གང་ལ་ལ་ཤེས་རབ་ཀྱི་ཕ་རོལ་ཏུ་
ཕྱིན་པ་ཟབ་མོའི་སྤྱོད་པ་སྤྱད་པར་འདོད་པ་དེས་འདི་ལྟར་རྣམ་པར་བལྟ་བར་བྱ་སྟེ། ཕུང་པོ་ལྔ་པོ་དེ་
དག་ཀྱང་། རང་བཞིན་གྱིས་སྟོང་པར་རྣམ་པར་ཡང་དག་པར་རྗེས་སུ་བལྟའོ། །

གཟུགས་སྟོང་པའོ། སྟོང་པ་ཉིད་གཟུགས་སོ། གཟུགས་ལས་སྟོང་པ་ཉིད་གཞན་མ་ཡིན།

སྟོང་པ་ཉིད་ལས་ཀྱང་གཟུགས་གཞན་མ་ཡིན་ནོ། དེ་བཞིན་དུ་ཚོར་བ་དང་། འདུ་ཤེས་དང་།

འདུ་བྱེད་དང་། རྣམ་པར་ཤེས་པ་རྣམས་སྟོང་པའོ། ཤཱ་རིའི་བུ་དེ་ལྟ་བས་ན་ཆོས་ཐམས་ཅད་སྟོང་པ་

ཉིད་དེ། མཚན་ཉིད་མེད་པ། མ་སྐྱེས་པ། མ་འགགས་པ། དྲི་མ་མེད་པ། དྲི་མ་དང་བྲལ་

བ་མེད་པ། བྲི་བ་མེད་པ། གང་བ་མེད་པའོ། ཤཱ་རིའི་བུ་དེ་ལྟ་བས་ན། སྟོང་པ་ཉིད་ལ་

གཟུགས་མེད། ཚོར་བ་མེད། འདུ་ཤེས་མེད། འདུ་བྱེད་རྣམས་མེད། རྣམ་པར་ཤེས་པ་མེད།

མིག་མེད། རྣ་བ་མེད། སྣ་མེད། ལྕེ་མེད། ལུས་མེད། ཡིད་མེད། གཟུགས་མེད།

སྒྲ་མེད། དྲི་མེད། རོ་མེད། རེག་བྱ་མེད། ཆོས་མེད་དོ། མིག་གི་ཁམས་མེད་པ་ནས།

ཡིད་ཀྱི་ཁམས་མེད། ཡིད་ཀྱི་རྣམ་པར་ཤེས་པའི་ཁམས་ཀྱི་བར་དུ་ཡང་མེད་དོ། མ་རིག་པ་མེད།

མ་རིག་པ་ཟད་པ་མེད་པ་ནས། རྒ་ཤི་མེད། རྒ་ཤི་ཟད་པའི་བར་དུ་ཡང་མེད་དོ། དེ་བཞིན་དུ

སྡུག་བསྔལ་བ་དང་། ཀུན་འབྱུང་བ་དང་། འགོག་པ་དང་། ལམ་མེད། ཡེ་ཤེས་མེད། ཐོབ

པ་མེད། མ་ཐོབ་པ་ཡང་མེད་དོ། ཤཱ་རིའི་བུ་དེ་ལྟ་བས་ན། བྱང་ཆུབ་སེམས་དཔའ་རྣམས་ཐོབ་པ་

མེད་པའི་ཕྱིར། ཤེས་རབ་ཀྱི་ཕ་རོལ་ཏུ་ཕྱིན་པ་ལ་བརྟེན་ཅིང་གནས་ཏེ། སེམས་ལ་སྒྲིབ་པ་མེད་པས་

སྐྲག་པ་མེད་དེ། ཕྱིན་ཅི་ལོག་ལས་ཤིན་ཏུ་འདས་ནས། མྱ་ངན་ལས་འདས་པའི་མཐར་ཕྱིན་ཏོ།

དུས་གསུམ་དུ་རྣམ་པར་བཞུགས་པའི་སངས་རྒྱས་ཐམས་ཅད་ཀྱང་། ཤེས་རབ་ཀྱི་ཕ་རོལ་ཏུ

ཕྱིན་པ་ལ་བརྟེན་ནས། བླ་ན་མེད་པ་ཡང་དག་པར་རྫོགས་པའི་བྱང་ཆུབ་ཏུ་མངོན་པར་རྫོགས་པར་

སངས་རྒྱས་སོ། དེ་ལྟ་བས་ན་ཤེས་རབ་ཀྱི་ཕ་རོལ་ཏུ་ཕྱིན་པའི་སྔགས། རིག་པ་ཆེན་པོའི་སྔགས།

བླ་ན་མེད་པའི་སྔགས། མི་མཉམ་པ་དང་མཉམ་པའི་སྔགས། སྡུག་བསྔལ་ཐམས་ཅད་རབ་ཏུ་ཞི

བར་བྱེད་པའི་སྔགས། མི་བརྫུན་པས་ན་བདེན་པར་ཤེས་པར་བྱ་སྟེ། ཤེས་རབ་ཀྱི་ཕ་རོལ་ཏུ་ཕྱིན་པའི

སྔགས་སྨྲས་པ། ཏདྱཐཱ། ཨོཾ་ག་ཏེ་ག་ཏེ་པཱ་ར་ག་ཏེ་པཱ་ར་སཾ་ག་ཏེ་བོ་དྷི་སྭཱཧཱ།

ཤུ་རིའི་བུ། བྱང་ཆུབ་སེམས་དཔའ་སེམས་དཔའ་ཆེན་པོ་ནི་ཤེར་ཤེས་རབ་ཀྱི་ཕ་རོལ་ཏུ་
ཕྱིན་པ་ཟབ་མོ་ལ་བསླབ་པར་བྱའོ། དེ་ནས་བཅོམ་ལྡན་འདས་ཏིང་ངེ་འཛིན་དེ་ལས་བཞེངས་ཏེ།
བྱང་ཆུབ་སེམས་དཔའ་སེམས་དཔའ་ཆེན་པོ་འཕགས་པ་སྤྱན་རས་གཟིགས་དབང་ཕྱུག་ལ་ལེགས་སོ་
ཞེས་བྱ་བ་བྱིན་ནས། ལེགས་སོ་ལེགས་སོ། རིགས་ཀྱི་བུ་དེ་དེ་བཞིན་ནོ། རིགས་ཀྱི་བུ་དེ་དེ་བཞིན་
ཏེ། ཇི་ལྟར་ཁྱོད་ཀྱིས་བསྟན་པ་དེ་བཞིན་དུ། ཤེས་རབ་ཀྱི་ཕ་རོལ་ཏུ་ཕྱིན་པ་ཟབ་མོ་ལ་སྤྱད་པར་བྱ་སྟེ།
དེ་བཞིན་གཤེགས་པ་རྣམས་ཀྱང་རྗེས་སུ་ཡི་རང་ངོ། བཅོམ་ལྡན་འདས་ཀྱིས་དེ་སྐད་ཅེས་བཀའ་སྩལ་
ནས། ཚེ་དང་ལྡན་པ་ཤ་རིའི་བུ་དང་། བྱང་ཆུབ་སེམས་དཔའ་སེམས་དཔའ་ཆེན་པོ་འཕགས་པ་སྤྱན་
རས་གཟིགས་དབང་ཕྱུག་དང་། ཐམས་ཅད་དང་ལྡན་པའི་འཁོར་དེ་དག་དང་། ལྷ་དང་། མི་
དང་། ལྷ་མ་ཡིན་དང་། དྲི་ཟར་བཅས་པའི་འཇིག་རྟེན་ཡི་རངས་ཏེ། བཅོམ་ལྡན་འདས་ཀྱིས་
གསུངས་པ་ལ་མངོན་པར་བསྟོད་དོ། འཕགས་པ་བཅོམ་ལྡན་འདས་མ་ཤེས་རབ་ཀྱི་ཕ་རོལ་ཏུ་ཕྱིན་པའི་
སྙིང་པོ་ཞེས་བྱ་བ་ཐེག་པ་ཆེན་པོའི་མདོ་རྫོགས་སོ།། ॥

རྒྱ་གར་གྱི་མཁན་པོ་བི་མ་ལ་མི་ཏྲ་དང་། ལོ་ཙྪ་བ་དགེ་སློང་རིན་ཆེན་སྡེས་བསྒྱུར་ཅིང་། ཞུ་
ཆེན་གྱི་ལོ་ཙྪ་བ་དགེ་སློང་ནམ་མཁའ་ལ་སོགས་པས་ཞུས་ཏེ་གཏན་ལ་ཕབ་པའོ། དཔལ་བསམ་ཡས་
ལྷུན་གྱིས་གྲུབ་པའི་གཙུག་ལག་ཁང་གི་དགེ་རྒྱས་བྱེ་མ་གླིང་གི་རྩིག་རྡོས་ལ་བྲིས་པ་དང་ཞུ་དག་ལེགས་
པར་བགྱིས་སོ།།

NOTES

Abbreviation: P: *Tibetan Tripiṭaka* (Tokyo-Kyoto: Tibetan Tripiṭaka Research Foundation, 1956)

[1] The Indian master Nagarjuna (Klu sgrub, first to second century) was the trailblazer who established the Madhyamika or Middle Way system of philosophical tenets which propound that while nothing has true existence, the conventional existence of actions and agents is feasible. His most famous work, the *Treatise on the Middle Way (Madhyamakaśāstra, dBu ma'i bstan bcos,* P5224, vol. 95), also called *Fundamental Wisdom (rTsa ba shes rab),* is a work in twenty-seven chapters which presents the explicit content of the Perfection of Wisdom sutras. It emphasizes dependent arising and explains the paths of insight related to the understanding of emptiness, employing a wide variety of approaches and lines of reasoning.

[2] *Bhagavatīprajñāpāramitāhṛdayasūtra, bCom ldan 'das ma shes rab kyi pha rol tu phyin pa'i snying po'i mdo,* P160, vol. 6. English translations: *Essence of the Heart Sutra: The Dalai Lama's Heart of Wisdom Teachings,* by Tenzin Gyatso the Fourteenth Dalai Lama, ed. and trans. Geshe Thupten Jinpa (Boston: Wisdom Publications, 2002); *The Key to the Treasury of Shunyata,* by Sermey Khensur Lobsang Tharchin (Howell, NJ: Mahayana Sutra and Tantra Press, 2002); *Elaborations on Emptiness: Uses of the Heart Sutra,* by Donald S. Lopez, Jr. (Princeton, NJ: Princeton University Press, 1996); *The Heart Sutra Explained: Indian and Tibetan Commentaries,* by Donald S. Lopez, Jr. (Albany, NY: State

University of New York Press, 1988); *Buddhist Wisdom: The Diamond Sutra and the Heart Sutra*, trans. and comm. by Edward Conze (New York: Vintage Books, 2001).

3 When the Buddha Shakyamuni came to our world from the Tushita pure land (dGa' ldan yid dga' chos 'dzin), Maitreya (rJe brtsun Byams pa) took over as its spiritual ruler. He will eventually manifest in this world as the next Buddha and display the deeds of a supreme emanation body (*mchog gi sprul sku*). It is said that if one hears and thinks about the five treatises, which he revealed to the great Indian master Asanga, one will be reborn in the Tushita pure land. In Tibet many of the largest statues were of Maitreya, who is represented sitting on a throne with his feet on the ground, ready to rise and come into the world. Just as Avalokiteshvara is the embodiment of perfect compassion, Maitreya is the embodiment of perfect love. His *Sublime Continuum of the Great Vehicle* (*Mahāyānottaratantraśāstra, Theg pa chen po rgyud bla ma'i bstan bcos*, P5525, vol. 108) has eight chapters: about the Buddha (*sangs rgyas*), the teachings (*chos*), the spiritual community (*dge 'dun*), the disposition (*khams*) (referring to Buddha nature), enlightenment (*byang chub*), qualities (*yon tan*), and enlightened activity (*phrin las*). The other four treatises are *Differentiating Phenomena and the Nature of Phenomena* (*Dharmadharmatāvibhaṅga, Chos dang chos nyid rnam par 'byed pa*, P5523, vol. 108); *Differentiating the Middle Way and the Extremes* (*Madhyāntavibhaṅga, dBus dang mtha' rnam par 'byed pa*, P5522, vol. 108); *Ornament for the Mahayana Sutras* (*Mahāyānasūtrālaṃkāra, Theg pa chen po'i mdo sde'i rgyan*, P5521, vol. 108), and the *Ornament for Clear Realization* (*Abhisamayālaṃkāra, mNgon par rtogs pa'i rgyan*, P5184, vol. 88).

4 The wheel of the teachings (*chos kyi 'khor lo*) symbolizes the transmission of the teaching from one person to another. The turning of the wheel sets the process in motion. The wheel also symbolizes the eightfold path of the exalted (*'phags lam yan lag brgyad*). Right speech (*yang dag pa'i ngag*), right action (*yang dag pa'i las kyi mtha'*) and right livelihood (*yang dag pa'i 'tsho ba*) are the hub, which represents the training in ethical discipline, the essential basis for the other two kinds of training. Right view (*yang dag pa'i lta ba*), right thought (*yang dag pa'i rtog pa*) and right effort (*yang dag pa'i rtsol ba*) are the sharp-edged

spokes, which represent the training in wisdom and the ability of analytical understanding to overcome everything discordant. Right mindfulness (*yang dag pa'i dran pa*) and right meditative stabilization (*yang dag pa'i ting nge 'dzin*) are the rim of the wheel, containing the mind and preventing it from wandering. This is the training in meditative stabilization.

[5] Aryadeva was the spiritual son of Nagarjuna and was active in the monastic university of Nalanda during the first half of the third century. His work *Four Hundred [Verses] on the Yogic Deeds of Bodhisattvas* (*Bodhisattvayogacaryācatuḥśatakaśāstra, Byang chub sems dpa'i rnal 'byor spyod pa bzhi brgya pa'i bstan bcos*, P5246, vol. 95) discusses the distorted ideas and disturbing emotions which prevent true Bodhisattva activity and the attainment of enlightenment. The first eight chapters of this work establish conventional reality, while the second eight establish ultimate reality by refuting various misconceptions regarding, for instance, the person, time, space, and matter. English translation: Geshe Sonam Rinchen and Ruth Sonam, *Yogic Deeds of Bodhisattvas: Gyeltsap on Aryadeva's Four Hundred* (Ithaca, NY: Snow Lion Publications, 1994).

[6] The Indian master Chandrakirti (Zla ba grags pa, seventh century) was the main spiritual son of Nagarjuna, whose works on sutra and tantra he elucidated and propagated. He lived in the monastic university of Nalanda and was an accomplished practitioner. He wrote the longest extant commentary (*Bodhisattvayogācaryacatuḥśatakaṭīkā, Byang chub sems dpa'i rnal 'byor spyod pa bzhi brgya pa'i rgya cher 'grel pa*, P5266, vol. 98) on Aryadeva's *Four Hundred [Verses] on the Yogic Deeds of Bodhisattvas.*

[7] Je Tsongkhapa (Tsong kha pa Blo bzang grags pa, 1357-1419), born in Amdo (A mdo), was a great reformer, dedicated practitioner and prolific writer. He founded Ganden Monastery (dGa' ldan rnam par rgyal ba'i gling) in 1409, the first of the monastic universities of the new Kadampa (bKa' gdams gsar ma) or Gelugpa (dGe lugs pa) tradition. His *Praise for Dependent Arising*, also known as the *Short Essence of Eloquence* (*rTen 'grel bstod pa* or *Legs bshad snying po chung ngu*, P6016, vol. 153) is a praise to the Buddha Shakyamuni for uniquely teaching dependent arising and emptiness. The lines cited here are from an

unpublished translation of Tsongkhapa's text, *Praise for Dependent Relativity,* by Ven. Graham Woodhouse, Buddhist School of Dialectics, Dharamsala, India. For another translation, see *The Key to the Treasury of Shunyata,* by Sermey Khensur Lobsang Tharchin (Howell, NJ: Mahayana Sutra and Tantra Press, 2002).

8   The great Indian masters Aryadeva ('Phag pa lha, c. second to third century), Buddhapalita (Sangs rgyas bskyangs, c. fifth to sixth century), Chandrakirti (Zla ba grags pa, seventh century) and Shantideva (Zhi ba lha, eighth century) commented, elucidated and expanded on Nagarjuna's presentation of Madhyamika philosophy based on the Perfection of Wisdom sutras.

9   Hearers (*snyan thos*) and Solitary Realizers (*rang sangs rgyas*) are intent on gaining personal liberation. They are practitioners of the Hinayana or Lesser Vehicle (*theg dman pa*), so called because their objective is limited to their own ultimate well-being. Practitioners of the Mahayana or Great Vehicle (*theg chen pa*), which consists of the Perfection Vehicle (*pha rol tu chin pa'i theg pa*) and the Secret Mantra Vehicle (*gsang sngags kyi theg pa*), aspire to attain complete enlightenment (*rdzogs pa'i byang chub*) for the sake of all beings and therefore have a considerably greater objective. The practices of the Lesser Vehicle, however, form the essential foundation for those of the Great Vehicle. Solitary Realizers accumulate more merit over a longer period than Hearers and do not depend upon the instructions of a spiritual teacher in their last rebirth before they attain liberation and become Foe Destroyers (*dgra bcom pa*)—those who have completely destroyed the disturbing emotions and their seeds. Practitioners of both the Lesser Vehicle and the Great Vehicle become exalted beings when they gain direct perception of reality.

10   Here "word" is used to translate *bka',* which is distinguished from the Buddha's speech (*gsung*), referring only to words spoken by the Buddha himself. The Buddha's word includes words added by the compiler of a particular sutra, referred to as permitted words (*rjes su gnang ba'i bka'*) and blessed words (*byin gyis brlabs pa'i bka'*), which the Buddha has inspired others to speak.

The Buddha's word is defined as scriptures of the Buddha (*sangs rgyas kyi gsung rab*) possessing four features: (1) The subject-matter deals with the qualities of high status (good rebirths), liberation, and so forth. (2) The words expressing this subject-matter are free from faults. (3) The function of the teaching is to enable one to get rid of whatever must be eliminated, namely the disturbing emotions of the three realms of existence (the desire, form, and formless realms) and so forth. (4) The purpose is to show the advantages of pacifying the disturbing emotions and suffering.

This definition is based on Maitreya's words in the *Sublime Continuum*:

> That which is meaningful, related to practice, and taught
> To eliminate the disturbing emotions of the three realms,
> That which shows the advantages of peace
> Is the Sage's word; the converse is other.

[11] The proponents of the four schools of Buddhist philosophical tenets are the Vaibhashikas (*bye brag smra ba*), the Sautrantikas (*mdo sde pa*), the Chittamatrins (*sems tsam pa*) and the Madhyamikas (*dbu ma pa*), consisting of the Svatantrikas (*rang rgyud pa*) and the Prasangikas (*thal 'gyur pa*). See Sopa and Hopkins, *Cutting Through Appearances: Practice and Theory of Tibetan Buddhism* (Ithaca, NY: Snow Lion Publications, 1989) for a succinct presentation of these systems of thought.

[12] Based on the Sanskrit language, names (*ming*) refer to uninflected stems, which do not indicate case, gender, number, etc. Words (*tshigs*) are inflected to indicate case, etc. Syllables (*yi ge*) are the basic building blocks for names and words.

Impermanent, produced or composite phenomena (*dus byas*), which exist through the coming together of the causes and conditions that produce them and which undergo change moment by moment, are of three types according to Buddhist philosophy. There are forms (*gzugs*), which include the five physical sense faculties and their objects. There are also forms, such as the objects which appear in our dreams, that are apprehended by mental consciousness. There are different kinds of awareness (*shes pa*), such as the five types of sense consciousness and mental consciousness as well as other types of mental activity. Lastly there are non-associated compositional factors (*ldan min 'du byas*), which are those impermanent phenomena that are neither form nor awareness. Included in this category are, for instance, the person, the life force, time, birth, and aging.

¹³ For an extensive refutation of permanent particles and time, see Aryadeva's *Four Hundred [Verses] on the Yogic Deeds of Bodhisattvas.* Permanent particles are refuted in the ninth chapter and truly existent time in the eleventh.

¹⁴ The wisdom truth body (*ye shes chos sku*) of an enlightened being results mainly from the great store of insight and embodies complete personal development. It is perceived only by other enlightened beings. The form bodies (*gzugs sku*) result primarily from the great store of merit and consist of the enjoyment (*longs sku*) and emanation bodies (*sprul sku*). These are manifestations of enlightened form for the benefit of others. The enjoyment body teaches continually and is perceived only by exalted beings. Emanation bodies are perceived by all those with the karmic predispositions to do so. The nature body (*ngo bo nyid sku*) of an enlightened being is the reality or emptiness of intrinsic existence of an enlightened being's mind.

¹⁵ Bya rgod phung po'i ri

¹⁶ Bodhgaya (rDo rje gdan), where the historical Buddha attained enlightenment, lies ninety kilometers south of the city of Patna in the modern Indian state of Bihar. The main Mahabodhi temple was originally built by a Ceylonese king. This is where the *bodhi* tree (*byang chub shing*) grows, said to be a descendant of the *Ficus religiosa* under which the Buddha sat in meditation. It is the most sacred place of pilgrimage for Buddhists from all over the world, and many temples representing the different Buddhist traditions have been built there.

¹⁷ In Tibetan these texts are known respectively as *'Bum* (*Śatasāhasrikāprajñāpāramitā*, P730, vol. 12), *Nyi khri* (*Pañcaviṃśatisāhasrikāprajñāpāramitā*, P731, vol. 18), and *brGyad stong pa* (*Aṣṭasāhasrikāprajñāpāramitā*, P734, vol. 21).

¹⁸ The *Ornament for Clear Realization,* one of Maitreya's five treatises, is a Mahayana text containing instructions on the hidden aspects of the Perfection of Wisdom sutras. The fact that there are twenty-one Indian commentaries on this work and many others by Tibetan masters indicates its great importance. Its subject-matter served as the basis for all the later Tibetan literature on the stages of the path.

¹⁹ The Indian master Vasubandhu (dByig gnyen) probably lived in the

fourth century. He is said to have held the Chittamatrin philosophical view but his *Treasury of Knowledge* (*Abhidharmakośa, Chos mngon pa'i mdzod*, P5590, vol. 115) is written from a Vaibhashika standpoint. It has eight chapters, of which the first three deal with the first noble truth, true suffering. The fourth chapter deals with actions as true sources of suffering and the fifth with the disturbing attitudes and emotions as true sources of suffering. This chapter also discusses true cessations, the third noble truth. The sixth chapter is about true paths, the fourth noble truth, and persons on the paths. The seventh chapter discusses different kinds of awareness, knowledge, and extrasensory perception. The eighth is about various states of absorption.

20 Chandrakirti's *Supplement to the Middle Way* (*Madhyamakāvatāra, dBu ma la 'jug pa*, P5261, P5262, vol. 98) is a commentary on the meaning of Nagarjuna's *Treatise on the Middle Way*, which it supplements with regard to the extensive aspect of practice. It deals with the ten Bodhisattva stages.

21 The monastic university of Nalanda, in what is now the Indian state of Bihar, was for many centuries the greatest center of secular and Buddhist studies in India. It was founded by King Kumaragupta in the fifth century and was later famed for its outstanding and vast library.

22 Kyabje Yongdzin Ling Rinpoche (sKyabs rje Yongs 'dzin gLing rin po che Thub bstan lung rtogs rnam rgyal 'phrin las, 1903-1984) was the senior tutor of His Holiness the fourteenth Dalai Lama. At the time of the Chinese invasion of Tibet the then Ganden Throne-holder (dGa' ldan khri pa) was unable to escape to India, and Kyabje Ling Rinpoche acted as his deputy. When the former Ganden Throne-holder died, Kyabje Ling Rinpoche became Ganden Throne-holder and remained in this office until his death.

Kyabje Yongdzin Trijang Rinpoche (sKyabs rje Yongs 'dzin Khri byang rin po che Blo bzang ye shes bstan 'dzin rgya mtsho, 1901-1981), was a close disciple of Pabongka Rinpoche (Pha bong kha rin po che, also known as Bla ma bDe chen snying po, 1878-1941) and belonged to the monastic university of Ganden. He was Junior Tutor to His Holiness the Dalai Lama.

23 *Mahāparinirvāṇasūtra, Yongs su mya ngan las 'das pa chen po'i mdo*, P787-789, vols. 30-31; *Ratnakūṭasūtra, dKon mchog brtsegs pa'i mdo*,

P760, vols. 22-24; *Buddhavatamsakasūtra, Sangs rgyas phal po che'i mdo,*
P761, vols. 25-26, also known as *mDo sde phal po che, Laṅkāvatārasūtra,
Lang kar gshegs pa'i mdo,* P775, vol. 29.

[24] *Ātajñānasūtra,' Da' ka ye shes,* P790, vol. 31; *Vajravidāraṇī, rDo rje rnam
par 'joms pa'i gzungs,* P406, vol. 8; *Samantabhadracaryāpraṇidhānarāja,
Kun tu bzang po spyod pa'i smon lam gyi rgyal po,* P716, vol. 11 (com-
monly known as *bZang spyod smon lam,* this is also found in the tantra
[rgyud] section of the *bKa' 'gyur); Āpattideśanā, lTung bshags,* also known
as the *Triskandhakasūtra, Phung bo gsum pa'i mdo,* P950, vol. 37.

[25] King Trisong Detsen (Khri srong sde btsan) ruled in the eighth century. The monastery of Samyey (bSam yas mi 'gyur lhun gyi grub pa'i
gtsug lag khang), where the first seven Tibetan monks were ordained,
was built during his reign. Nyangkhampa or Langkhampa (rLangs
kham pa Go cha bya ba) had perfected the ability to retain in his mind
what he memorized without forgetting it (*mi brje pa'i gzungs*).

[26] Geshe Sharawa (dGe bshes Sha ra ba, also Shar ba pa, 1070-1141)
was ordained by the great Kadampa (bKa' gdams pa) master Geshe
Potowa (dGe bshes Po to ba Rin chen gsal, 1031-1105) and had more
than three thousand students, many of whom came to him after Geshe
Potowa passed away. He had good knowledge of Sanskrit and super-
vised revisions of earlier translations with which he was not satisfied.
He taught the essentials of how to transform one's way of thinking to
Geshe Chekawa (dGe bshes mChad kha ba, 1101-1175), who later
wrote the famous text *Seven Points for Training the Mind (Blo byong
don bdun ma).*

[27] The *Great Exposition of the Stages of the Path (Lam rim chen mo,*
P6001, vol. 152) sets out in detail the complete path to enlightenment
in terms of three levels of capacity. It is richly adorned with quotation
both from the sutras and from the works of the great Indian masters.
It is the longest of Tsongkhapa's works on the stages of the path. Translation by the Lamrim Chenmo Translation Committee, *Great Treatise
on the Stages of the Path* (Ithaca, NY: Snow Lion Publications, 2000,
2002).

[28] *Nagas (klu)* are said to be serpentine creatures, belonging to the realm
of animals, who live in water. Some have a jewel on the crown of their

heads. The more important *nagas* live in seas and oceans and own palaces and fabulous wealth. Lesser *nagas* live in springs and lakes. If one's conduct pleases them, they send or stop rain, whichever is needed. They like cleanliness and take offence when their dwelling places are polluted. As a result they may cause skin and other diseases. The Mahayana teachings are said to have been given into their safekeeping.

29 The Sanskrit syllables *Om Mani Padme Hung* form the mantra of Avalokiteshvara, the embodiment of enlightened compassion. The mantra is primarily associated with the four-armed form of the deity, who holds a string of crystal prayer beads and the stem of a lotus. There are many interpretations of this profound mantra. In Ngulchu Dharmabhadra's (dNgul chu dharma bhadra, 1772-1851) *Heart Wealth of Bodhisattvas* (*rGyal sras snying nor*), a commentary on Geshe Chekawa's *Seven Points for Training the Mind*, the following brief interpretation occurs: the syllable *Om* serves as an invocation. *Mani* means jewel and signifies skillful means, such as love and compassion, while *Padme* means lotus and signifies wisdom. *Hung* is the seed syllable of enlightened mind. Avalokiteshvara combines perfected skillful means and wisdom. Thus the mantra can be interpreted as a request, "You who hold the jewel and the lotus, please look on me with compassion and bless me to become like you."

30 The conventional spirit of enlightenment (*kun rdzob byang chub kyi sems*) is the consciousness accompanying the intention to become enlightened for the sake of all living beings. The ultimate spirit of enlightenment (*don dam byang chub kyi sems*) is the direct understanding of reality, namely that all phenomena are empty of inherent existence, supported by this intention.

31 *theg mchog la mos sa pon / shes rab ni sang rgyas chos skyed ma dang*

32 The Sanskrit word *bhagavatī* and the Tibetan *bcom ldan 'das ma*, translated as "the Victorious," both display feminine gender markers.

33 Non-abiding nirvana (*mi gnas pa'i myang 'das*) refers to the highest state of enlightenment (*rdzogs pa'i byang chub*) in which one is free from the fears associated with both worldly existence and personal peace (*srid zhi 'jigs pa las grol ba*). Worldly existence is compared to a sea of poison and personal peace likened to an ocean of milk.

34 The essence of those who have gone to bliss (*bde bar gshegs pa'i snying po*) or the essence of those thus gone (*de bzhin gshegs pa'i snying po*) is generally referred to as Buddha nature (*sangs rgyas kyi rigs*) in English.

35 *rang bzhin myang 'das*

36 The minds of living beings and of Buddhas are both equally free from natural stains (*rang bzhin gyi dri ma*), namely the stains of true existence. This is natural purity (*rang bzhin rnam dag*). However, because the mind itself (the entity of the mind: *sems kyi ngo bo*) is affected by temporary stains (*glo bur gyi dri ma*), consisting of the disturbing attitudes and emotions as well as their imprints, the way that living beings see things is affected by appearances of true existence.

Since our minds and these stains are constantly and closely associated, we are unable to see the reality of the mind, which is like the sky covered by clouds. While we are unable to engage with the reality of our minds directly and can only do so by way of terms (a sound image, *sgra spyi*) or by way of a mental image (*don spyi*), we are still ordinary beings (*so so skye bo*). From the path of seeing until the final moment as a Bodhisattva just prior to enlightenment we have the ability to see reality directly while in meditative equipoise, but there are still stains which prevent us from entering into meditative equipoise on the reality of the mind and never arising from it again. Thus although the stains are not an integral part of the mind's nature (*rang bzhin*), here referring to its ultimate nature, they affect or pollute the entity (*ngo bo*) of the mind, namely the mind itself, which is clear and cognizant.

When enlightenment is attained, the natural purity and the purity of temporary stains come together. Thus one can refer to the nature body which is natural purity (*rang bzhin rnam dag ngo bo nyid sku*) and the nature body which is the purity of temporary stains (*glo bur rnam dag ngo bo nyid sku*), but these are merely different terms referring to the same thing. In the enlightened state the mind (*sems kyi ngo bo*) engages with its own nature (*sems kyi rang bzhin*), its emptiness, in such a way that one will never arise from that state again. This is why it is said that the stains have vanished within the sphere of emptiness. The disappearance of clouds is not something separate from the sky or space in which they vanish and which is a mere absence of obstruction. Similarly, separation from the adventitious stains is not something separate from emptiness, the natural purity.

That which is nirvana (*myang 'das*) is also true cessation (*'gog bden*) but not all true cessations are nirvana. When, for instance, the objects of elimination by the path of seeing have been completely eliminated, a true cessation is attained but this is not nirvana, which at the very least is the total separation from all disturbing attitudes and emotions and their seeds, temporary stains that form obstructions to liberation (*nyon sgrib*). When the obstructions to knowledge of all phenomena (*shes sgrib*) have been removed, non-abiding nirvana (*mi gnas pa'i myang 'das*), the state of highest enlightenment, is attained.

[37] Panchen Sönam Drakpa (Pan chen bSod nams grags pa, 1478-1554) was the author of the textbooks used by Loseling College of Drepung Monastery ('Bras spung Blo gsal gling) and by Shardzey College of Ganden Monastery (dGa' ldan Shar rtse).

[38] The four features characterizing the disposition of the exalted (*'phags pa'i rigs bzhi*) are contentment with poor clothing (*chos gos ngan ngon tsam gyis chok shes pa*), contentment with meager alms (*bsod snyoms ngan ngon tsam gyis chok shes pa*), contentment with a poor dwelling (*gnas mal ngan ngon tsam gyis chok shes pa*), and a liking for getting rid of what needs to be discarded and for meditation (*spong ba dang sgom pa la dga' ba*).

[39] The followers of scripture (*lung gi rjes 'brangs*) are those mainly relying upon the works of the Indian master Asanga, while the followers of reasoning (*rigs pa'i rjes 'brangs*) mainly rely upon the works of the Indian masters Dignaga and Dharmakirti. The latter posit five kinds of sense consciousness (*dbang shes*) and mental consciousness (*yid shes*), while the former posit eight kinds of consciousness: the five kinds of sense consciousness, mental consciousness, foundational consciousness (*kun gzhi*), and afflicted mind (*nyon yid*). Afflicted mind mainly consists of misconceptions of the self. Foundational consciousness, which is unobstructed and neutral, carries the imprints of past virtuous and non-virtuous actions.

[40] The seeds of uncontaminated mind: *zag med sems kyi sa bon,* or the potential for uncontaminated mind: *zag med sems kyi nus pa.*

The Heart Sutra

[41] The developmental disposition: *rgyas 'gyur gyi rigs.* The naturally abiding or innately abiding disposition: *rang bzhin gnas rigs.*

[42] In Tibetan the definition of the innately or naturally abiding disposition (*rang bzhin gnas rigs*) is *rang gi rten chos dri ma dang bcas pa'i sems kyi chos nyid ngo bo nyid sku 'gyur rung.* The definition of the developmental disposition (*rgyas 'gyur gyi rigs*) is ' *dus byas su gyur pa'i sangs rgyas kyi sku 'gyur rung.* A product (*'dus byas*) is that which has come into existence through causes and conditions and which changes moment by moment.

[43] For instance, the *Tathāgatasaṃgītisūtra* (P895, vol. 35) consists of three sections of twenty-five verses each.

[44] *shes rab pha rol tu phyin pa*

[45] Chittamatrins assert that what is apprehended (*bzung ba*) and the apprehending awareness (*'dzin pa*) both come into being from the same imprint on consciousness. They therefore say that apprehended objects and apprehending subjects are not separate entities (*bzung 'dzin rdzas tha dad med pa* or *bzung 'dzin gnyis su med pa*). The exalted understanding of this is referred to as *bzung 'dzin gnyis su med pa'i ye shes.*

[46] The wisdom truth body (*ye shes chos sku*), which is the culmination of an enlightened being's personal development, has two aspects: perfect elimination (*spang pa phun tshogs*) and perfect realization (*rtogs pa phun tshogs*). A fully enlightened one's elimination of what must be overcome has three features. (1) Non-Buddhist ascetics who are free from attachment have temporarily suppressed this and other manifest disturbing emotions but have not yet rid themselves of their seeds. They also still have manifest wrong views of the self (*bdag lta*). However, an enlightened being has completely and excellently eliminated (*legs par spang pa*) all misconceptions of the self, as well as all disturbing emotions and their seeds. (2) Exalted practitioners of the Lesser Vehicle, who are still on the paths of training, such as those who abide in the fruit of a stream-enterer and others, have rid themselves of intellectually formed views of the self and their seeds but are not yet rid of the innate wrong views of the self and their seeds. Because of this the disturbing emotions can arise again and activate karmic imprints that will lead to rebirth in cyclic existence. Enlightened beings have eliminated

everything that could make them return to cyclic existence. This is irreversible elimination (*slar mi ldog par spang pa*). (3) Foe Destroyers of the Lesser Vehicle still have imprints of the disturbing emotions, which can cause them to perform faulty physical actions, whereas fully enlightened beings have rid themselves completely (*ma lus pa spang pa*) of these imprints. These three features are also referred to as excellently gone to bliss (*legs par bde gshegs*), irreversibly gone to bliss (*slar mi ldog par bde gshegs*) and completely gone to bliss (*ma lus par bde gshegs*). Collectively they are elimination that has gone to bliss (*spang pa bde gshegs*).

The perfect realization of an enlightened one is referred to as realization that has gone to bliss (*rtogs pa bde gshegs*) and is also characterized by three features. (1) It is superior to the understanding of non-Buddhists because it is a realization of suchness (*de kho na nyid mkhyen pa*). (2) Since stream-enterers of the Lesser Vehicle have not yet rid themselves of the seeds of the wrong view of the self, their knowledge is not stable. Enlightened ones have rid themselves fully of these seeds and perfectly understand reality, so that their realization is stable (*mkhyen pa brtan pa*) and irreversible (*slar mi ldog pa'i mkhyen pa*). (3) Unlike the Foe Destroyers of the Lesser Vehicle, enlightened ones have complete realization (*ma lus par mkhyen pa*) because they know the entire paths of the Hearer, Solitary Realizer, and Great Vehicles and can teach them to those with the three kinds of disposition.

[47] The Indian master Haribhadra (Seng ge bzang po) lived in the late eighth century. He was born into a royal family but took ordination. He is said to have studied the Madhyamika view with the famous scholar Shantirakshita (Zhi ba 'tsho), who is also known as the great Bodhisattva Abbot (mKhan chen Bo dhi sa ttva) because he travelled to Tibet to ascertain whether it was feasible to ordain monks there and subsequently ordained the first group at Samyey Monastery (bSam yas). Haribhadra became a renowned scholar of the Perfection of Wisdom sutras and wrote a commentary on Maitreya's *Ornament for Clear Realization* known as the *Clear Meaning Commentary* (*Abhisamayālamkāraprajñāpāramitopadeśaśāstravrtti, Shes rab kyi pha rol tu phyin pa'i man ngag gi bstan bcos mngon par rtogs pa'i rgyan kyi 'grel pa*, also called *'Grel pa don gsal*, P5191, vol. 90). Like Maitreya's *Ornament*, which it elucidates, it explains the hidden content of the

Perfection of Wisdom sutras and is highly valued by Tibetan scholars for its conciseness and clarity. The statements regarding Ananda are made in Haribhadra's extensive commentary on Maitreya's *Ornament*, which is also a commentary on the *Perfection of Wisdom Sutra in Eight Thousand Verses* (*Aṣṭasāhasrikāprajñāpāramitāvyākhyānābhisamayālaṃkārāloka*, *Shes rab kyi pha rol tu phyin pa brgyad stong pa'i bshad pa mngon par rtogs pa'i rgyan gyi snang ba*, also known simply as *rGyan snang* in Tibetan, P5189, vol. 90).

[48] Ananda (Kun dga' bo) was one of the Buddha Shakyamuni's closest disciples and eventually became his personal attendant. He is said to have had an outstanding memory and during the first council, shortly after the Buddha passed away, he was able to recite by heart many teachings of the Buddha, which were compiled at that time. There is a touching story about Ananda's devotion to the Buddha. One day, during a time of famine, they had been invited to a meal. Their host, who was a trader, served up a dish of beans that did not taste good. The tears came to Ananda's eyes at the thought that the Enlightened One was being offered such poor food. Seeing this, the Buddha took a bean from his mouth and gave it to Ananda to taste. To his amazement the taste was divine!

[49] The Indian master Bhavaviveka (Legs ldan 'byed) lived in the sixth century. He was born in south India and studied at the monastic foundation at Magadha, close to Bodhgaya. He was a great exponent of Madhyamika philosophy and wrote a famous text called the *Heart of the Middle Way* (*Madhyamakahṛdaya*, *dBu ma'i snying po*, P5255, vol. 96) as well as a commentary on this text known as the *Blaze of Reasoning* (*Madhyamkahṛdayavṛttitarkajvālā*, *dBu ma'i snying po'i 'grel pa rtog ge 'bar ba*, P5256, vol. 96), in which he expresses the opinion that the Bodhisattvas Samantabhadra, Manjushri, Vajrapani, and Maitreya compiled the basis of the Mahayana sutras. Bhavaviveka also wrote a famous commentary on Nagarjuna's *Treatise on the Middle Way*. The general tenets of the Svatantrika school of Madhyamika philosophy and in particular those of the Sautrantika-Svatantrika branch are based on his writing.

[50] Vajrapani is one of the eight Bodhisattvas known as the eight close sons of the Buddha (*nye ba'i sras brgyad*). Though they have the same

qualities and powers, each displays perfection in one particular area or activity: Manjushri ('Jam dpal dbyangs) embodies wisdom; Avalokiteshvara (sPyan ras gzigs) embodies compassion; Vajrapani (Phyag na rdo rje) represents power; Kshitigarbha (Sa'i snying po) increases the richness and fertility of the land; Sarvanivarana Vishkambhin (sGrib pa rnam sel) purifies wrong-doing and obstructions; Maitreya (Byams pa) embodies love; Samantabhadra (Kun tu bzang po) displays special expertise in making offerings and prayers of aspiration; Akashagarbha (Nam mkha'i snying po) has the perfected ability to purify transgressions. While the Buddha was still alive, he gave Vajrapani, who had exceptional powers of memory, the authority to compile the teachings and it is said that he was the chief compiler of the secret mantra teachings.

[51] Bimbisara was the king of Magadha at the time of the Buddha Shakyamuni. Bodhgaya, where the Buddha manifested the deed of attaining enlightenment, was situated in his kingdom. At the age of thirty Bimbisara heard the Buddha teach and became his devoted follower. He presented the bamboo grove of Venuvana to the Buddha, who then often taught his followers there. Bimbisara was later murdered by his son Ajatashatru. When Ajatashatru was king, he was afflicted by a terrible skin disease and covered with stinking pustules, which burned so fiercely that even those standing close to him could feel the heat. In desperation he eventually turned to the Buddha for help. He took the teachings he received to heart and through his sincere practice was able to purify himself and attain great insights.

On one occasion Ajatashatru invited the Buddha and his followers for a meal. In the company of the Buddha was the Bodhisattva Manjushri, in whom Ajatashatru had great faith and for whom he had prepared some beautiful clothes. When he was about to offer the clothes, Manjushri suddenly vanished and the king felt regret that he had missed this opportunity. At that very moment he felt as if he himself were vanishing too. Because he already had the predispositions for it, this induced an understanding of emptiness. The virtue created by his faith and by preparing the fine clothes to offer to Manjushri and then Manjushri's disappearance provided the circumstances which activated those predispositions.

[52] Kushinagar (rTswa mchog drong), now Kasia in the modern Indian

state of Uttar Pradesh, is where the Buddha passed away in his eightieth year. Some of the Buddha's relics were enshrined in a great stupa there. For many centuries it was an important place of pilgrimage with many sacred shrines and monasteries, but it was already in a state of neglect by the seventh century, so the Chinese pilgrim and scholar Hsüan-tsang reported, and little remains to be seen today.

53 *Śālistambhasūtra, Sa lu'i ljang pa'i mdo,* P876, vol. 34.

54 Rajgir (Rājagrha) in Tibetan is *rGyal po'i khab,* literally the residence of the king. It is said that the Buddha frequently taught in a great mango grove near Rajgir that belonged to a wealthy surgeon called Jivaka, who was his devoted follower.

55 There are eight kinds of individual liberation vow (*so sor thar pa'i sdom pa rigs brgyad*). The individual liberation vow (*so thar gyi sdom pa*) is so called because observing it enables an individual to attain liberation. It focuses primarily on the maintenance of pure physical and verbal conduct. Different forms of this vow are taken by lay and ordained people. The "vow of one who remains nearer" (*bsnyen gnas kyi sdom pa*), through which one draws closer to liberation, is taken for only twenty-four hours at a time and is therefore not considered equal to the others as a basis for the Bodhisattva vow. It consists of restraint from (1) killing, (2) stealing, (3) lying, and (4) sexual activity. One may not use (5) high or fancy seats or (6) intoxicants, (7) eat after midday, (8) wear garlands, jewelry, or perfume, make music, dance, or sing. This vow is taken by lay persons.

The second and third kinds of individual liberation vow, which are also taken by lay persons, are the "vow of one close to virtue" (*dge bsnyen gyi sdom pa*) for men and for women. Virtue here refers to nirvana. Both men and women vow to observe restraint from (1) killing, (2) stealing, (3) lying, and (4) sexual misconduct. They also promise to refrain from the use of intoxicants.

The remaining kinds of individual liberation vow are taken by those who leave family life behind (*rab tu byung ba*). They must rely on an abbot, give up the signs of lay life, adopt the signs of ordained life, and insure that they do not deviate from these three forms of conduct. The fourth and fifth kinds are "vows of those entering the path to virtue" (*dge tshul gyi sdom pa*), often referred to as novice monks' and nuns' vows. They involve restraint from (1) killing, (2) stealing, (3) lying, (4) sexual activity, (5) making music, dancing, or singing, (6) wearing garlands, jewelry, or perfume, (7) accepting silver or gold with the intention of keeping them, (8) taking food after midday, and (9) using ornate seats or (10) high seats.

The sixth is the "vow of a female trainee in virtue" (*dge slob ma'i sdom pa*). In preparation for becoming a fully ordained nun she must hold the vow of a novice nun and in addition practice restraint from twelve activities for two years. She must not (1) travel unless accompanied by someone who observes a similar code of discipline, (2) swim naked across a big river to reach the other side, (3) touch a man, (4) sit on the same seat as a man, (5) act as a matchmaker, (6) hide the transgressions of a female friend, (7) own gold or other valuables, (8) shave her pubic hair, (9) eat what has not been given to her, (10) eat food she has saved, (11) cut green grass and dispose of bodily excretions indiscriminately, or (12) dig the earth.

The seventh and eighth kinds are the "vows of those who strive for virtue" (*dge slong gi sdom pa* and *dge slong ma'i sdom pa*). A fully ordained nun must refrain from three hundred and sixty-four activities; a fully ordained monk from two hundred and fifty-three.

⁵⁶ Mahakashyapa ('Od srung chen po) was renowned for his great self-discipline and excellent ethics. After the Buddha passed away, he became the leader of the spiritual community.

⁵⁷ The sixteen Foe Destroyers or elders (*gnas brtan bcu drug*, literally "sixteen stable ones" or "sixteen who are firm in their place") are Angaja (Yan lag 'byung), Ajita (Ma pham pa), Vanavasin (Nags na gnas), Kalika (Dus ldan), Vajriputra (rDo rje mo'i bu), Bhadra (bZang po), Kanakavatsa (gSer gyi be'u), Kanaka Bharadvaja (Bha ra rdwa dza gser can), Bakula (Ba ku la), Rahula (sGra can 'dzin), Chudapanthaka (Lam phran bstan), Pindola Bharadvaja (Bha ra rdwa dza bsod snyoms len), Mahapanthaka (Lam chen bstan), Nagasena (Klu'i sde), Gopaka (sBed byed), and Abheda (Mi phed pa). There is a very well-known prayer in Tibetan called *Homage and Offerings to the Elders* (*gNas brtan phyag mchod*) which describes the location of each, how many Foe Destroyers surround him and what hand gesture he is making or what he holds. They have vowed to remain in their different places, protecting the teachings of the Buddha Shakyamuni for as long as they last.

[58] The jewel of the spiritual community (*dge bdun dkon mchog*) refers in its narrowest sense to all exalted beings, whether ordained or lay, who have reached the path of seeing and have thus had direct experience of reality.

[59] Avalokiteshvara, Chenrezig (sPyan ras gzigs) in Tibetan, here appears as a Bodhisattva and one of the Buddha's close disciples. He also appears as an enlightened being and meditational deity, embodying enlightened compassion. Iconographically he is most often depicted in a four-armed and in a thousand-armed form. The latter has eleven heads: the top head is the red face of Amitabha Buddha in an emanation body form with a crown protrusion and no jewels. Below this is a fierce black face with fangs, glaring eyes and flaming tresses. Below this are three heads; the central one is red, that to its left is white and that to its right is green. Below these are three more heads which are, in the same order, green, red and white respectively. Below these are three more: white, green and red respectively. These nine heads all have peaceful eyes.

The first two hands touch at the heart with a hollow between them symbolizing the form and wisdom bodies of enlightened beings. The second right hand holds crystal prayer beads, representing skillful means. The third right hand is in the gesture of supreme giving. From it flows nectar alleviating the hunger and thirst of hungry ghosts. This gesture denotes the promise to bestow everything that is needed, and the common as well as powerful attainments. The fourth right hand holds a wheel which denotes the uninterrupted turning of the wheel of teaching for living beings.

The second left hand holds an unsullied lotus to show that Chenrezig is untainted by any trace of selfishness. It also represents wisdom. The third left hand holds a water pot to symbolize the washing away of all disturbing attitudes and emotions. The fourth holds a bow and arrow to show that by teaching living beings he will lead them to the path that combines skillful means and wisdom. The other nine hundred and ninety-two arms and hands symbolize his ability to emanate universal monarchs. The eyes in the palms of the hands represent the ability to emanate the thousand Buddhas of the fortunate era. All this is for the benefit of living beings.

[60] The five aggregates (*phung po lnga*) are form (*gzugs kyi phung po*),

feeling (*tshor ba'i phung po*), recognition (*'du shes kyi phung po*), compositional factors (*'du byed kyi phung po*), and consciousness (*rnam shes kyi phung po*). The twelve sources (*skye mched bcu gnyis*) are form (*gzugs*), sound (*sgra*), smell (*dri*), taste (*ro*), tangible objects (*reg bya*), and phenomena (*chos*) as well as the visual faculty (*mig gi dbang po*), the auditory faculty (*rna ba'i dbang po*), the olfactory faculty (*sna'i dbang po*), the gustatory faculty (*lce'i dbang po*), the tactile faculty (*lus kyi dbang po*), and the mental faculty (*yid kyi dbang po*). The eighteen constituents (*khams bcu brgyad*) are all of the former as well as the six kinds of consciousness which arise in dependence on them: visual consciousness (*mig gi rnam shes*), auditory consciousness (*rna ba'i rnam shes*), olfactory consciousness (*sna'i rnam shes*), gustatory consciousness (*lce'i rnam shes*), tactile consciousness (*lus kyi rnam shes*), and mental consciousness (*yid kyi rnam shes*).

[61] *'Phags pa* is the short form of *khyad par du 'phags pa*, which means exalted, transcendent, or superior.

[62] The five paths are the path of accumulation (*tshogs lam*), the path of preparation (*sbyor lam*), the path of seeing (*mthong lam*), the path of meditation (*sgom lam*), and the path of no more learning (*mi slob lam*). One enters the Hinayana path of accumulation when the thought to free oneself from cyclic existence is constantly present. One enters the Mahayana path of accumulation and becomes a Bodhisattva when the spirit of enlightenment is spontaneously and constantly present. At this point one begins to accumulate the great stores of merit and insight necessary for the attainment of enlightenment. The path of preparation, marked by the union of a calmly abiding mind and special insight focusing on emptiness, prepares one for the direct perception of reality. This is the first time that one develops the understanding of emptiness derived from meditation. When direct perception of reality is achieved, one becomes an exalted being and attains the path of seeing and the first Bodhisattva stage. On the path of meditation the Mahayana practitioner gains ever-increasing familiarity with the direct perception of emptiness and practices the perfections, eliminating more and more subtle obstructions to enlightenment. When all of these have been removed, one attains the path of no more learning and becomes an enlightened being.

The path of preparation has four phases during which the veils to direct perception of emptiness formed by the mental image of emptiness are gradually removed. Heat (*drod*) is a sign that the fire of the non-conceptual understanding of emptiness will soon burn brightly. Peak (*rtse mo*) is the stage where the virtue one has created becomes stable and can no longer be damaged by wrong views. Patience (*bzod pa*) marks a lack of fear of and ability to tolerate emptiness. One will never again take a bad rebirth as a result of contaminated actions underlain by the disturbing emotions. Supreme mundane qualities (*'jig rten pa'i chos kyi mchog*, usually referred to as supreme qualities, *chos mchog*) marks the highest level of realizations of an ordinary person as opposed to those of an exalted one.

[63] dGe bshes Klu sgrub thabs mkhas. Sera Monastery (Se ra theg chen gling) was founded in 1419 by Jamchen Chöjey Shakya Yeshey (Byams chen chos rje Sha'kya ye shes).

[64] Construction of Norbulingka (Nor bu gling kha), the summer residence of the Dalai Lamas just outside the periphery of Lhasa proper, which is marked by the outer circumambulation route (*gling 'khor*), began during the reign of the seventh Dalai Lama, Kelsang Gyatso (bsKal bzang rgya mtsho, 1708-1757), with the building of the first palace, called bsKal bzang pho brang. Successive Dalai Lamas built residences on this site which eventually formed a complex of beautiful palaces. The surrounding area was a favorite place for picnics.

[65] The full title is *Essence of Eloquence, a Treatise Discriminating the Interpretable and the Definitive* (*Drang ba dang nges pa'i don rnam par phye ba'i bstan bcos legs par bshad pa'i snying po*, P6142, vol. 153. English translation: Robert Thurman, *Tsong Khapa's Speech of Gold in the Essence of True Eloquence*, Princeton: Princeton University Press, 1984). In this text Je Tsongkhapa distinguishes between those statements by the Buddha that are definitive and those that require interpretation. He explains this from the point of view of the Chittamatra, Svatantrika, and Prasangika schools, and in doing so fully elucidates their philosophical positions.

[66] The Mahayana disposition (*theg pa chen po'i rigs*) is awakened when we develop great compassion (*snying rje chen po*), the wish to free all

living beings without exception from suffering. Taking heartfelt refuge again and again acts as one of the causes for the disposition to awaken.

67 The Mongolian scholar Tendar Lharampa (bsTan dar lha ram pa) was born in 1759. The last work of his for which a date is known was written in 1839, indicating that he lived beyond the age of eighty. He was a disciple of Longdöl Lama (Klong grol bla ma). His commentary on the *Heart Sutra, Jewel Light Illuminating the Meaning* (*Shes rab snying po'i grel pa don gsal nor bu'i 'od*), is one of the main sources for this oral teaching.

68 From a Prasangika point of view, those sutras which primarily explain emptiness are definitive (*nges don*), while those which primarily explain the conventional are interpretable (*drang don*). Here the distinction is made with respect to subject-matter. Concerning the expression of that subject-matter, those statements which can be taken literally are definitive whereas those which cannot are interpretable. Teachings which help those for whom they are specifically intended to enter the paths are interpretable. Those which directly help them to attain the result are definitive. Proponents of philosophical tenets define sutras which accord with their view as definitive and sutras which do not as interpretable. In general, however, the classification of definitive and interpretable is made primarily with reference to subject-matter.

69 The three doors are the door of emptiness (*sgo stong pa nyid*), the door of signlessness (*mtshan ma med pa'i sgo*), and the door of wishlessness (*smon pa med pa'i sgo*).

70 The ten Bodhisattva stages are called very joyful (*rab tu dga' ba*), stainless (*dri ma med pa*), luminous (*'od byed pa*), radiant (*'od 'phro ba*), difficult to overcome (*sbyang dka' ba*), approaching (*mngon du phyogs pa*), gone afar (*ring du song ba*), immovable (*mi g.yo ba*), good intelligence (*legs pa'i blo gros*), and cloud of the teachings (*chos kyi sprin*). On all of these stages during meditative equipoise on emptiness there is no difference in focal object nor in the way the mind apprehends its object. The differences lie in the varying accomplishments and abilities accompanying these stages. Each stage has its particular qualities

(*yongs sbyong*) which enable faults to be overcome and accomplishments to be gained. On each stage Bodhisattvas gain expertise in a particular practice.

Respectively these practices are giving (*sbyin pa*), ethical discipline (*tshul khrims*), patience (*bzod pa*), enthusiastic effort (*brtson 'grus*), concentration (*bsam gtan*), wisdom (*shes rab*), skillful means (*thabs*), prayer (*smon lam*), power (*stobs*), and exalted knowledge (*ye shes*). Bodhisattvas practice all of these perfections on every stage.

71 Gungtang Könchok Tenpey Drönmey (Gung tang dKon mchog bstan pa'i sgron me, 1762-1823), also known as Manjushri of Gungtang (Gun tang 'Jam dpal dbyangs), from the Amdo (A mdo) region of eastern Tibet, was a disciple of the second Jamyang Sheypa, Könchok Jigmey Wangpo ('Jam dbyangs bzhad pa dKon mchog 'jigs med dbang po). Among his best known works are a study of the four truths, commentaries on Tsongkhapa's work on the foundational mind (*kun gzhi*) and on his *Essence of Eloquence* (*Legs bshad snying po*), and a short text on the three doors to liberation. His commentary on the *Heart Sutra's* mantra is called *Illuminating the Hidden Meaning* (*Shes rab snying po'i sngags kyi rnam bshad sbas don gsal ba sgron me*).

Donald Lopez's book *The Heart Sutra Explained* (Albany, NY: State University of New York Press, 1988) contains translations of Tendar Lharampa's commentary as well as Gungtang Rinpoche's commentary. It also examines seven Indian commentaries on the *Heart Sutra* by Vimalamitra, Jnanamitra, Vajrapani, Prashastrasena, Kamalashila, Atisha, and Mahajana. Tendar Lharampa's commentary draws primarily on Vimalamitra, Prashastrasena, and Mahajana, while Gungtang follows the commentaries of Vimalamitra and Atisha most closely.

72 There are five omnipresent factors (*kun 'gro*): feeling (*tshor ba*), discrimination ('*du shes*), intention (*sems pa*), contact (*reg pa*), attention (*yid la byed pa*).

Five determining factors (*yul nges*): aspiration ('*dun pa*), belief (*mos pa*), mindfulness (*dran pa*), stabilization (*ting nge 'dzin*), knowledge (*shes rab*).

Eleven virtuous mental factors (*dge ba*): faith (*dad pa*), self-respect (*ngo tsha shes pa*), decency (*khrel yod*), non-attachment (*ma chags pa*), non-hatred (*zhe sdang med pa*), non-confusion (*gti mug med pa*), effort (*brtson 'grus*), mental pliancy (*shin tu sbyangs ba*), conscientiousness (*bag yod*), equanimity (*btang snyoms*), non-violence (*rnam par mi 'tshe ba*).

Six basic disturbing attitudes (*rtsa nyon*): desire (*'dod chags*), anger (*khong khro*), pride (*nga rgyal*), ignorance (*ma rig pa*), doubt (*the tshom*), deluded views (*lta ba nyon mongs can*).

Twenty secondary disturbing attitudes (*nye nyon*): aggression (*khro ba*), resentment (*'khon 'dzin*), concealment (*'chab pa*), spite (*'tshig pa*), jealousy (*phrag dog*), miserliness (*ser sna*), deceit (*sgyu*), dissimulation (*g.yo*), inflation (*rgyags pa*), violence (*rnam par 'tshe ba*), lack of self-respect (*ngo tsha med pa*), inconsideration (*khrel med pa*), lethargy (*rmugs pa*), excitement (*rgod pa*), lack of faith (*ma dad pa*), laziness (*le lo*), lack of conscientiousness (*bag med pa*), forgetfulness (*brjed nges pa*), lack of alertness (*shes bzhin med pa*), distraction (*rnam par g.yeng ba*).

Four changeable factors (*gzhan 'gyur*) which may be positive or negative: sleep (*gnyid*), regret (*'gyod pa*), investigation (*rtog pa*), analysis (*dpyod pa*).

[73] This is the twelve-part process by which we remain in cyclic existence taking one involuntary rebirth after another. The twelve links of dependent arising (*rten 'brel yan lag bcu gnyis*) are normally enumerated in the following order: ignorance (*ma rig pa*), formative action (*'du byed*), consciousness (*rnam par shes pa*), name and form (*ming gzugs*), the sources (*skyed mched*), contact (*reg pa*), feeling (*tshor ba*), craving (*sred pa*), grasping (*len pa*), existence (*srid pa*), birth (*skye ba*), aging and death (*rga shi*).

[74] The ten powers (*stobs bcu*) of an enlightened one are the power of knowing what is a cause and what is not a cause for a particular result (*gnas dang gnas min mkyen pa'i stobs*); the power of knowing the maturation of actions (*las kyi rnam par smin pa mkyen pa'i stobs*); the power of knowing different interests (*mos pa sna tshogs mkyen pa'i stobs*); the power of knowing different dispositions (*khams sna tshogs mkyen pa'i stobs*); the power of knowing different faculties (*dbang po sna tshogs mkyen pa'i stobs*); the power of knowing the paths to all goals, such as what paths lead to a good rebirth, to liberation, or to complete enlightenment (*thams cad du 'gro ba'i lam mkyen pa'i stobs*); the power of knowing what kinds of meditative absorptions rid one of which disturbing emotions and the purified results they bring (*kun nas nyon mongs pa*

dang rnam par byang ba mkyen pa'i stobs); the power of knowing past lives (*sngon gyi gnas rjes su dran pa mkyen pa'i stobs*); the power of knowing in what realm of existence death occurred and in what realm birth will occur (*'chi 'pho ba dang skye ba mkyen pa'i stobs*); the power of knowing the end of all contamination (*zag pa zad pa mkyen pa'i stobs*).

The four kinds of fearlessness (*mi 'jigs pa bzhi*) of an enlightened being are fearlessness in asserting that one has eliminated everything that must be eliminated for one's own good (*rang don du spangs pa thams cad spangs zhes dam bcas pa la mi 'jigs pa*), fearlessness in asserting that one possesses all the qualities needed for one's own good (*rang don du yon tan thams cad dang ldan zhes dam bcas pa la mi 'jigs pa*), fearlessness in asserting for the good of others what the counteractive paths are (*gzhan don du gnyen po'i lam 'di dag go dam bcas pa la mi 'jigs pa*), and fearlessness in asserting for the good of others what needs to be eliminated (*gzhan don du 'di dag spang bya yin dam bcas pa la mi 'jigs pa*).

[75] According to the Svatantrikas the distinction between selflessness of persons and selflessness of phenomena is based on what is negated, whereas for Prasangikas what is negated in both cases is the same—true or inherent existence—and the distinction is made in terms of the basis of selflessness. For the Svatantrikas the misconception of the person as truly existent is the conception of a self of phenomena and is an obstruction to knowledge of all phenomena. The understanding that there is no truly existent person is the understanding of the subtle selflessness of phenomena.

According to the Svantantrika view the table is empty of a self of persons because it is not an object of use by a self-sufficient substantially existent person and also empty of a self of phenomena because it is not truly existent, i.e. it does not exist exclusively from its own side without appearing to non-defective awareness, which is their criterion for true existence.

[76] The fundamental middle: *gzhi dbu ma*; the middle path: *lam dbu ma*; the resultant middle: *'bras bu dbu ma*. In addition to this there is the textual middle (*gzhung dbu ma*), which refers to texts dealing with the Madhyamika view.

[77] The different categories of tantra are defined in relation to how much desire the practitioner can handle and use as a path of practice. Action

tantra (*bya rgyud*) is for those who can make use of the desire aroused by looking at the consort but who cannot control stronger desire. Performance tantra (*spyod rgyud*) is for those capable of utilizing the desire aroused by smiling at and flirting with the consort, and yoga tantra (*rnal 'byor rgyud*) for those who can harness the desire which arises from touching and embracing. These are all acts of imagination. Highest yoga tantra (*rnal 'byor bla med rgyud*) is for those who can control the desire generated by actual contact between the sexual organs. From the point of view of the emptiness cognized and the deity yoga practiced, there is no difference between these different categories of tantra.

Action tantra involves mainly external rituals like the observance of certain dietary rules and bathing. Performance tantra combines such external rituals with the practice of meditative stabilization. Yoga tantra focuses primarily on internal practices, and highest yoga tantra involves the subtlest and most advanced of these.

According to some interpretations, "with signs" refers to deity yoga practiced without the understanding of emptiness, while "without signs" connotes such practice accompanied by the understanding of emptiness. However, it is always said that in order to practice tantra effectively, one needs a sound basis of the three principal aspects of the path: the wish to be free from cyclic existence, the spirit of enlightenment, and the understanding of emptiness. In theory, therefore, all genuine tantric practice will be based on some understanding of emptiness.

In his *Great Exposition of Secret Mantra* (*sNgags rim chen mo*, P6210, vol. 161) Je Tsongkhapa defines "with signs" and "without signs" as deity yoga and mantra recitation unaccompanied by or accompanied by meditation on emptiness. Practice "without signs" here refers to the yoga of non-dual profundity and clarity (*zab gsal gnyis med kyi rnal 'byor*), which begins by meditating on emptiness that appears as a vacuity from which the deity arises. Then, taking the visualized deity as the basis, one meditates on the emptiness of what is appearing. It is a conceptual state of mind to which both the deity, the basis of emptiness, and its emptiness of inherent existence, namely its fundamental nature, appear simultaneously. This constitutes the inseparable combination of skillful means and wisdom in a single awareness. Both the perception of the deity and of its fundamental nature manifest together.

According to this explanation, practice with signs may or may not be supported by the understanding of emptiness. When it is, meditation on emptiness precedes visualization of the deity, and the force of this understanding of emptiness informs what follows but is not actually part of the awareness apprehending the deity.

[78] The great seal: *phyag rgya chen po*; the teaching or speech seal: *chos kyi phyag rgya*; the commitment seal: *dam tshig gi phyag rgya*; the action seal: *las kyi phyag rgya*.

[79] In tantra the stage of generation (*bskyed rim*) is practiced to overcome ordinary appearances and one's clinging to them. Ordinary appearances are counteracted by imagining oneself as the deity and one's surroundings as the celestial mansion and other components of the mandala. One's clinging to such ordinary appearances is countered by strong identification with the deity. Practices during the stage of completion (*rdzogs rim*) involve focusing intense attention on the energy channels, energy winds, and drops of the subtle body, particularly at the different centers, to activate the most subtle level of awareness and to generate great bliss. This blissful awareness is eventually used to apprehend emptiness, the clear light (*'od gsal*), and to produce the illusory body (*sgyu lus*).

[80] Thorough training of the Bodhisattva stages: *sa'i yongs sbyong*.

[81] The false view of the transitory collection: *'jig tshogs la lta ba*; holding misleading forms of discipline and conduct as supreme: *tshul khrims dang brtul zhugs mchog 'dzin*; deluded doubt: *the tshom nyon mongs can*.

[82] Vimalamitra was the Indian scholar with whom, as was customary, Rinchen Dey (Rin chen sde) collaborated during the translation of the *Heart Sutra*. He was born in western India in the eighth century and studied in Bodhgaya as well as in China. He was invited to Samyey (bSam yas) Monastery during the reign of King Trisong Detsen (Khri srong lde btsan) where he taught on the sutras and tantras, wrote commentaries mainly on tantra, and translated texts from Sanskrit into Tibetan in partnership with Tibetan translators. He played a key role in establishing the Great Completion (*rdzogs chen*) teachings in Tibet. His commentary on the *Heart Sutra* (*Prajñāpāramitāhrdayaṭīkā, Shes rab kyi pha rol tu phin pa'i snying po'i rgya cher bshad pa*, P5217, vol.

94) is the longest of the extant Indian commentaries. No information is at present available on the translators Rinchen Dey and Namka (Nam mkha').

[83] Samyey Monastery (bSam yas mi 'gyur lhun gyi grub pa'i gtsug lag khang), the first monastery in Tibet, was built during the reign of Trisong Detsen (Khri srong lde btsan, eighth century). It is said to have been modeled on an Indian monastery called Ogyenpuri (O rgyan pu ri), probably Odantapuri, and that while Samyey was under construction, the work done by the builders during the day was destroyed by hostile spirits at night. This continued until Padmasambhava blessed the monastery, after which the spirits became so cooperative that they carried on building during the night. The bottom storey was constructed of stone in the Tibetan style. The middle storey was built of bricks in the Chinese style and the top storey was made of wood in the Indian style.

The first seven Tibetan monks were ordained there as an experiment to see whether Tibetans were capable of observing the individual liberation vow. Many early translations were completed and revised at Samyey, whose library contained many precious treasures. The contents of this library were dispersed during the Cultural Revolution, when many volumes were taken to Beijing.

The temple of Geygyey Chema Ling (dGe rgyas bye ma gling) was founded by one of Trisong Detsen's queens, Tsünmo Tri Gyelmo Tsen (bTsun mo Khri rgyal mo btsan), who took ordination as a nun and was then known as Jangchup Jey (Byang chub rje).

SOURCE READINGS

Commentaries in Tibetan that served as a basis for this teaching:

Shes rab snying po'i 'grel pa don gsal nor bu'i 'od
by Ngag dbang bstan dar lha ram pa, 1759-?. The last of his works for
which a date is known was written in 1839.

Shes rab snying po'i sngags kyi rnam bshad sbas don gsal ba sgron me
by Gung thang dKon mchog bstan pa'i sgron me, 1762-1823

Shes rab snying po'i 'grel pa
by 'Bras spungs sgo mang mkhan zur Ngag dbang nyi ma, 1907-1990

Shes rab snying po'i sbas don mngon rtogs kyi rim pa gsal ba'i nyi ma
by 'Brong rtse Yongs 'dzin Blo bzang tshul khrims, 1745-1800

In English:

The Heart Sutra Explained
by Donald S. Lopez, Jr. (Albany: State University of New York Press,
1988)

Printed in the United States
By Bookmasters